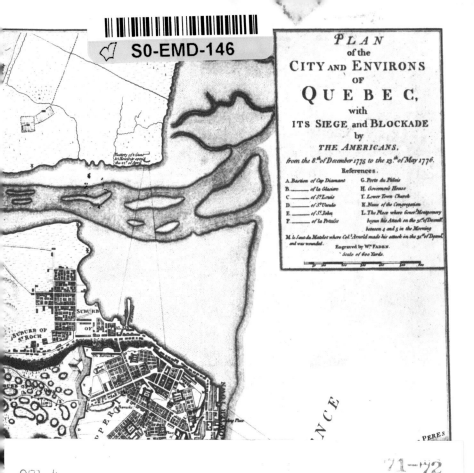

PLAN
of the
CITY AND ENVIRONS
OF
QUEBEC,
with
ITS SIEGE and BLOCKADE
by
THE AMERICANS.

from the 8.ᵗʰ of December 1775 to the 13.ᵗʰ of May 1776.

References.

A. Bastion of Cap Diamant   G. Porte du Palais
B. _____ of la Glacière   H. Governors House
C. _____ of St Louis   Y. Lower Town Church
D. _____ of St Ursule   K. Nuns of the Congregation
E. _____ of St John   L. The Place where Genrl Montgomery
F. _____ of la Potasse   begun his Attack on the 31 of Decemr
between 4 and 5 in the Morning

M. le Sant du Matelot where Col. Arnold made his attack on the 31 of Decemr
and was wounded.   Engraved by Wm FADEN.
Scale of 600 Yards.

Ainslie, Thomas.

   Canada preserved; the journal of Captain Thomas Ainslie. Edited by Sheldon S. Cohen. ₍New York₎ New York University Press ₍ᶜ1968₎

   vi, 106 p. illus., map. 22 cm. 5.00

   "Journal of the most remarkable occurrences in the Province of Quebec from the appearance of the Rebels in September 1775 until their retreat on the sixth of May."
   "Original manuscript ... is on deposit at the Houghton Library of Harvard University."
   Includes bibliographical references.

   1. Quebec (City)— Siege, 1775–1776.   I. Cohen, Sheldon S., ed.
II. Title.

E231.A62   971.4′02   500
                                                  69–13117
                                                  MARC

Library of Congress   .12₎

Canada Preserved

Canada Preserved

The Journal of Captain Thomas Ainslie

Edited by
SHELDON S. COHEN

New York University Press

Library of Congress Catalogue Card Number 69-13117

CONTENTS

ACKNOWLEDGEMENTS

I extend my appreciation to the following institutions for their generous advice and assistance:

Archives of the Ministère des Affaires Culturelles du Quebec; The British Museum; Cour Supérieure, Montreal and Quebec; The Houghton Library, Harvard University; The Library of Congress; The Literary and Historical Society of Quebec; The National Maritime Museum, Greenwich, England; The New-York Historical Society; The New York Public Library; Prothonotaries of Judicial Archives, Montreal and Quebec; The Public Archives of Canada; Public Record Office, London; Public Record Office of Northern Ireland, Belfast; Rhodes House Library, Oxford University; The Yale University Library; The Yale University Art Gallery.

INTRODUCTION

The conquest of Canada had been a prime military concern of American settlers throughout the later Colonial period. From the final decades of the seventeenth century onward, colonial statemen—and particularly New Englanders—had urged the destruction of New France.[1] Intermittent European wars between England and France served as a backdrop to years of bitter and bloody conflict in North America. King William's War (1689-97), Queen Anne's War (1702-13), King George's War (1744-8), and the beginning of the French and Indian War in 1754 passed with France still controlling its strategic citadels along the St. Lawrence. At last, in 1759, General Wolfe's memorable victory on the Plains of Abraham had signalled the fall of Quebec, and four years later the American Colonists rejoiced over Canada's cession to Great Britain by the Peace of Paris.[2]

Such decisive developments were not to be the final military struggles over Canada. Less than six months after the Revolutionary War erupted at Lexington and Concord, American forces began their major attempts to wrest Canada from British control. As early as May 1775, a small group of patriots under Vermont farmers, Ethan Allen and Seth Warner, and a former New Haven apothecary, Benedict Arnold, captured the important fortresses

---

[1]Justin H. Smith, *Our Struggle For the Fourteenth Colony* (New York, 1907), I, 21-3, Jeremiah Dummer, "A Memorial shewing that the French Possessions on the River of Canada do originally and of right belong to the Crown of Great Britain . . .," Mass. Hist. Soc., *Collections*, 3rd Ser., I (1846), 231-234.

[2]Howard H. Peckham, *The Colonial Wars* 1689-1762 (Chicago, 1964), pp. vii-240; Edward P. Hamilton, *The French and Indian Wars* (Garden City, 1962), pp. xii-318.

1

of Ticonderoga and Crown Point on Lake Champlain.[3] The St. Lawrence Valley was opened for invasion and, despite the Second Continental Congress' initial declaration that "it had nothing more in view than the defense of these Colonies," strategic and political opportunities proved too tempting. Delegates such as Samuel Adams and Benjamin Franklin considered Canada a natural and integral part of any united American state, and they also feared that any reinforced British Army would be certain to use this northern springboard to crush their nascent rebellion.[4]

As a result, Congress soon began to retreat from its original declaration. The climax was reached on June 25, 1775, when instructions were approved for Major General Philip Schuyler at Fort Ticonderoga, stating that if the General found it "practicable, and that it will not be disagreeable to the Canadians, he shall immediately take possession of St. John's, Montreal, and any other parts of the country."[5]

General Schuyler proved exceedingly dilatory in his task and his second-in-command, Brigadier General Richard Montgomery, gradually assumed responsibility for preparing the initial thrust into Canada. Unlike the aristocratic and spiritless Schuyler, Montgomery was bold, energetic and had acquired a notable military background while serving under General Jeffrey Amherst in the French and Indian War.[6]

[3]John R. Alden, *The American Revolution* 1775-1783 (New York, 1954), pp. 47-48; Smith, II, 121-44.

[4]Worthington C. Ford *et al*, eds., *Journals of the Continental Congress, 1774-1789* (Washington, 1904-37), II, 75; Claude H. Van Tyne, *The War for Independence, The American Phase* (Cambridge, 1929), II, 69; Richard B. Morris and Henry C. Commanger, eds., *The Spirit of Seventy-Six* (New York, 1958), I, 184; Arnold Whitridge, "Canada, The Struggle for the Fourteenth State," *History Today*, XVII No. 1 (January, 1967), 13-15.

[5]*Journals of the Continental Congress*, II, 109-10.

[6]See James T. Adams in *DAB* s.v. "Montgomery, Richard"; *Dictionary of American Biography* (New York, 1936), XIII, 98-9; Smith, *op cit.*, I, 367-70, 610. (Montgomery was born in 1736 in Swords County, Ireland. He had entered the Army in 1754 and during the French and Indian War he served at the siege of Louisbourg and apparently at the capture of Montreal in 1760. In 1772, he resigned his commission as captain and migrated to America, where he married a member of the Livingston family and settled on a farm near Rhinebeck, New York.)

Experienced as he was, Montgomery found himself severely limited, not only by his lethargic commander but also by a shortage of supplies, ill-trained troops, and the divisive spirit of intercolonial jealousies. Yet, somehow, his personal energy and enthusiasm mitigated these deficiencies, and by the first week in September 1775 American forces were moving northward along Lake Champlain. On September 16 illness forced Schuyler's retirement from the scene and Montgomery achieved full command.[7]

Within nine weeks, this seventeen-hundred-man expedition had overcome rugged British resistance and achieved its initial objectives. The surprisingly strong defense of the outnumbered redcoats was directed by Governor Guy Carleton who, like Montgomery, was an Irish-born veteran of the French and Indian conflict. At the outbreak of hostilities, Carleton commanded only four infantry regiments scattered as far as the Great Lakes and, in addition, faced a prevalent threat of subversion from disgruntled French Canadian peasants (habitants) as well as several pro-patriot merchants.[8]

Although the Governor had wisely declared martial law in early June and had issued urgent appeals for volunteers from among the populace, most Canadians, aside from the landowning seigneurs, remained indifferent to his appeals. By the beginning of Montgomery's advance Carleton could muster only six hundred men to garrison Fort St. Johns, his principal defensive position below Montreal.

There Major Charles Preston made a stubborn stand but was surrounded and obliged to capitulate on November 3. Ten days later, Montreal's alarmed inhabitants forced the surrender of the town to the advancing Americans. Montgomery entered in triumph the next day while Carleton, who had fled up-river, was barely able to escape a trap near Sorel which snared most of his remaining troops and ships.[9]

---

[7]Allen French, *The First Year of the American Revolution* (Cambridge, 1934), pp. 383-416; Smith, *op. cit.*, I, 247-67, 335.

[8]Smith, *op. cit.*, I, 99-103, 201-2, 304-5. Carleton, (1724-1808), was born in Strabane County, Ireland, not far from Montgomery's home.

[9]Alden, pp. 51-52, 55; Smith, *op cit.*, I, 342-7, 433-48, 455-66, 470-90.

3

Somewhat simultaneously with Montgomery's advance a second American force invaded Canada and descended upon Quebec by the more direct but also more dangerous Kennebec-Chaudière River route. The one thousand men who began the march in late September had been detached from General Washington's troops besieging Boston.

Benedict Arnold, now a Continental Army colonel, directed the men as they moved along the treacherous Kennebec River in Maine. When they left the Kennebec to portage via the Dead River and Lake Megantic, the expedition almost ended in disaster. Food shortages, illness, accidents and some nearly impassable terrain disheartened the men to such an extent that the three rear companies and their commander abandoned the struggle. Isolated, existing largely on dog-meat and boiled roots and threatened with extinction, the remainder of Arnold's dwindling expedition groped forward in a spirit mixing courage with desperation. On October 30 a ragged and exhausted advance party reached the first French Canadian settlements along the Chaudière where the surprised but sympathetic habitants reacted with immediate aid to all the stragglers. Arnold and the other survivors rested briefly. Then, with about five hundred men, he pushed toward the mouth of Chaudière and on November 8 reached Point Levis opposite Quebec.[10]

Arnold's troops succeeded in crossing the St. Lawrence after a six-day delay, but the arrival of over one hundred Loyalist reinforcements under Lieutenant Colonel Allan Maclean on November 12 had already saved the citadel from the "weak and diffident" command of Lieutenant Governor Hector Cramahé. With Governor Carleton's dramatic return on the 19th, Arnold's

---

[10]Kenneth L. Roberts, ed., *March to Quebec: Journals of the Members of Arnold's Expedition Compiled and Annotated by Kenneth Roberts During the Writing of Arundel* (New York, 1938), pp. xiv-657; Lynn Montross, *Rag Tag and Bobtail, The Story of the Continental Army 1775-83* (New York, 1952), pp. 52-55; Justin H. Smith, *Arnold's March from Cambridge to Quebec* (New York, 1903), pp. xix-498; Smith, *Our Struggle for the Fourteenth Colony*, I, 603-6.

immediate threat receded and the Americans withdrew a short distance down-river.[11]

Events soon led to a new crisis for the garrison. While Carleton hurriedly strengthened the town's physical defenses and augmented his garrison with Canadian militiamen, disembarked sailors, marines, and volunteer residents, Arnold and Montgomery were consolidating their available forces.

For Montgomery this proved a difficult task. The imminent expiration of enlistments and petty dissensions enabled him to assemble less than four hundred men by November 28 when his fleet of ships sailed from Montreal. Some additional Canadian sympathizers, recruited by Major James Livingston, joined the expedition at Sorel and on December 2 Montgomery's units formally linked up with Arnold at Aspen Point, twenty miles above Quebec. After his own men were disembarked and Arnold's chilled troops supplied with captured British uniforms, the combined forces moved immediately and enthusiastically upon Quebec.

Early on the morning of December 5 they were encamped before the imposing citadel—the last British stronghold in Canada.[12]

It was at Quebec, however, that the American drive was thwarted and the ambitions of Congress were shattered. Faced with this new American threat Governor Carleton judiciously decided to remain under siege behind the town's strengthened fortifications and to await reinforcements from England. When Montgomery proved unable to pressure his numerically superior opponent into combat or cajole him into surrender, he decided to storm the town before too many enlistments expired. Plans for the assault were carefully laid despite the inexperience of many of his officers.

[11]The Case of Lieutenant John Starke of His Majesties Navy. MS 149/129, BRG/9 Archives of the National Maritime Museum, Greenwich, England; Alden, pp. 54-5; Smith, *Our Struggle for the Fourteenth Colony,* II, 5-10, 21-31.

[12]French, pp. 430-42; Smith, *Our Struggle for the Fourteenth Colony,* II, 74-91, 577.

The attack was launched during a pre-dawn snowstorm on December 31. Two feints were made against the town's outer gates while separate groups under Arnold and Montgomery made the principal attacks from opposite sides of the Lower Town. It proved to be a valorous but abortive assault for the Americans. Montgomery and two of his aides were cut down by a cannon blast from an armed guardhouse, while Arnold was carried away wounded after bravely penetrating one of the outer barriers on the other side of town. Most of General Montgomery's troops retreated immediately after his death, but Arnold's men, now led by Captain Daniel Morgan, fought on desperately until cut off and forced to surrender. At the conclusion of the battle the Americans had lost sixty to seventy men killed and wounded plus four hundred taken prisoner, while Carleton's defenders counted five dead and fourteen wounded.[13]

Despite such a severe setback the Americans maintained a desultory siege of Quebec throughout the winter and into the spring. The initial decision was made by the wounded Colonel Arnold, who stubbornly refused to accept defeat and pleaded with Congress and General Washington for more supplies and reinforcements.[14]

Although new troops and more money were requisitioned and eventually trickled into the American positions, the bitterly cold winter and the constant presence of pestilence took their toll of the besiegers. Men froze at their posts. By March the number of smallpox victims in hospitals neared four hundred. As a result,

[13]Peter Force, ed., *American Archives: Fourth Series, Containing a Documentary History of the English Colonies in North America from the King's Message to Parliament of March 7, 1774 to the Declaration of Independence by the United States* (Washington, 1837-46), IV, 187-91, 288-9; William H. Smith, *History of Canada from Its First Discovery to the Year 1791* (Quebec, 1815), II, 92-137; Piers Mackesy, *The War for America* 1775-83 (Cambridge, 1964), pp. 79-89; Smith, *Our Struggle for the Fourteenth Colony*, II, 98-143.

[14]Alden, p. 57; Smith, *Our Struggle for the Fourteenth Colony*, II, 153-7. In March 1776, several of the captured American prisoners plotted to escape and throw open the main gates to the besiegers. The plan, however, was soon discovered and most of the ring-leaders placed in irons. Smith, *op. cit.*, II, 277-93; Ainslie Journal, Entry for March 31, 1776.

John Trumbull

DEATH OF GENERAL MONTGOMERY

the actual American threat to Quebec proved rather minimal following the year-end assault. In spite of some inconveniences and hardships, morale remained high among Carleton's defenders, while Arnold's successors, Generals David Wooster and John Thomas, faced the constant problem of desertion. By the beginning of May only about 1900 sick and weary patriot troops remained in loosely-held positions around the town.[15]

Soon afterward British reinforcements finally arrived and the Americans were quickly and firmly routed. As early as February, 1776, Lord George Germain, the Minister of War, had answered Carleton's urgent appeals for assistance by dispatching a troop convoy from England under Sir Charles Douglas. Two months later General Sir William Howe sent a regiment from Halifax, but both relief expeditions were delayed by adverse weather conditions and obstructive ice floes in the St. Lawrence River.[16] Their arrival on the morning of May 6 was greeted with unrestrained jubilation by the defenders. The same day the weakened besiegers were easily scattered by a sortie from the town.

Overnight the formerly indifferent or hostile habitants emerged with a display of support for the royal cause and proclamations of disdain for the invaders. The American retreat turned into a rout, especially following another defeat at Three Rivers on June 7. Eight days later Montreal was hastily evacuated, and by the end of the month the Americans had been completely expelled from Canada.[17]

[15]Alden, pp. 57-58; Smith, *Our Struggle for the Fourteenth Colony*, II, 181-313.

[16]Lord George Germain to Governor Guy Carleton, February 17, 1776, Canadian Archives, Q, 12, p. 1; General Sir William Howe to the Secretary of State, April 25, 1776; Public Record Office, America and West Indies, Volume 305, p. 265; Smith, *Our Struggle For the Fourteenth Colony*, II, 294-7.

[17]French, pp. 695-7, Smith, *Our Struggle for the Fourteenth Colony*, II, 319-458 (In March, Congress sent a commission, consisting of Benjamin Franklin, Charles Caroll and Father John Carroll to Canada in order to gain the support of the French Canadians. The commission was rebuffed and the members fled from Montreal immediately following the relief of Quebec). See Smith, *Our Struggle For the Fourteenth Colony*, II, 325-43.

The significance of the valiant but inglorious campaign often lacks the attention it deserves in general surveys of American history. One recent study of bias in Anglo-American text books noted that American junior high school texts gave scant attention to the unsuccessful invasion, and high school histories rarely pointed out the American mistakes in launching their campaign against Quebec.[18] Yet the campaign did have its historical consequences.

First, it undoubtedly marked the closest the United States came to seizing Canada. Had Quebec fallen to Arnold and Montgomery, its retention would certainly have proven difficult, but capture of this strong fortress might well have stymied any relief force. Of related significance was the fact that the American invasion of Canada had delayed the British counterthrusts into America. Restoring stability in the recaptured areas of Canada delayed Governor Carleton's counter-invasion into New York until the late summer of 1776, giving the patriots ample time to strengthen their defenses and build a flotilla on Lake Champlain.[19]

Secondly, the campaign served as a training ground for the Continental Army, if nothing else. Battle-tested leaders like Daniel Morgan, Jonathan Meigs, John Sullivan and even Benedict Arnold had emerged from the expedition hardened by the dangers of combat. For many of the surviving Americans the vigorous suffering and bitter privations of winter were to be repeated at places like Valley Forge and Morristown. Truly, it was to be a long road from the freezing frustrations outside Quebec to the glorious autumn triumph at Yorktown in 1781, but American patriots had shown that they possessed the determination and fortitude to endure the journey.

There are several manuscript accounts, American and British, of the Canadian campaign and the siege of Quebec. The American journals of officers like Simeon Thayer, Henry Dearborn,

---

[18]Ray A. Billington *et al.*, *The Historian's Contribution to Anglo-American Misunderstanding, Report of a Committee on National Bias in Anglo-American History Textbooks* (London, 1966), pp. 41, 53.
[19]Smith, *Our Struggle for the Fourteenth Colony*, II, 462-3.

Jonathan Meigs and Doctor Isaac Senter offer a good description of the earlier phases of the campaign, but they become conspicuously weaker in narrating the events at Quebec.[20] In contrast the British accounts of the invasion written by officers such as Hugh Finlay, Sir John Hamilton, and Henry Caldwell center primarily on the seige of Quebec.[21] Probably the best British narrative in this latter respect was written by Thomas Ainslie. Some of the details of Ainslie's early life are incomplete. Though the origin of the surname (Anesley, Anslee, Aynesley) can be traced to both Medieval England and Scotland, by the early eighteenth century it was found to be most common in the border settlements of southern Scotland.[22] Quite possibly Thomas Ainslie came to America from this region as a youth in 1748. In April, 1762, he was appointed collector of customs for Quebec with the approval of the military governor, General James Murray. Prior to the American Revolution, he was involved in several disputes with local merchants and Governor Carleton, who once questioned Ainslie's integrity and his raising of fees without reference to the home Government.[23]

[20]Simeon Thayer's Journal, Rhode Island Historical Society *Collections,* VI. (1867), 1-104; Journal of Captain Henry Dearborn, Mass., Hist. Soc., Proceedings, (1886), 275-305; Return Jonathan Meigs, *Journal of the Expedition Against Quebec* . . . (New York, 1864), vi, 7-57; Isaac Senter, *The Journal of Isaac Senter Physician and Surgeon* . . . Reprinted from the Historical Society of Pennsylvania (Tarrytown, N. Y., 1915), pp. 1-60.

[21]"Hugh Finlay's Journal of the Siege and Blockade of Quebec, by the American Rebels in Autumn 1775 and Winter 1776." Literary and Historical Society of Quebec, *Historical Documents*, 4th Ser. (1875), pp.3-25; William T. P. Short, ed., *Journal of the Principal Occurrences During the Siege of Quebec by the American Revolutionists Under Generals Montgomery and Arnold* (London, 1824), pp. 1-45 (Attributed to Sir John Hamilton); Major Henry Caldwell to General James Murray, June 15, 1776, Literary and Historical Society of Quebec, *Manuscripts Relating to the Early History of Canada*, 2nd Series, V, 9-13.

[22]George F. Black, *The Surnames of Scotland* (New York, 1946), p. 12.

[23]Robert Willcocks, Merchant, v Thomas Ainslie, Court of Common Pleas, District of Quebec June 17, 1774, T.I./515 Public Record Office; Governor Guy Carleton to the Secretary of State, July 5, 1770, January 12, 1775, MG 11, Series Q 11, pp. 122-5, 152; Thomas Ainslie to Governor Carleton's Secretary October 10, 1770, MG 11, Series Q 8, pp. 2-7;

Despite such quarrels Ainslie was a staunch Loyalist like most British customs officials, and, when the Americans invaded Canada, he volunteered to defend Quebec. He was given the temporary rank of Captain with the British militia and served as a company commander throughout the siege of the town.[24] The duties which Thomas Ainslie performed were apparently his only military functions during the war. In August, 1778, the newly appointed Canadian Governor-General, Sir Frederick Haldimand, denied his request for a grant of land within the town of Quebec.[25]

Meanwhile, Ainslie continued in his position as collector of customs—though once again difficulties arose during his tenure of office. At least one member of his staff was accused of neglect of duty and a dispatch sent to Governor Dorchester (Sir Guy Carleton) in 1789 suggested the need for a stricter audit of Ainslie's accounts. This may have accounted for the fact that he had been previously recommended unsuccessfully for a seat on the Governor's council.[26] After 1799 Ainslie was no longer mentioned in the annual list of collectors of customs. Little is known of his family life, although his first wife Mary died in 1767 at age 25, and during the last decade of the century his residence was listed as No. 1 Ste. Anne Street. Thomas Ainslie himself apparently lived to a ripe old age, although no exact date of his death has been located in Quebec or Montreal.[27]

Application of Thomas Ainslie, April 16, 1786, MG 11, Series Q 26-1, pp. 249-50, Public Archives of Canada, Ottawa.

[24]"Orderly Books of Captains Anthony Vialar and Robert Lester," Literary and Historical Society of Quebec, *Historical Documents*, 7th Ser. (1905), pp. 155-265.

[25]Thomas Ainslie to Governor Sir Frederick Haldimand, August 5, 1778, Haldimand to Ainslie August 6, 1778, MG 21, B 200-2, pp. 539-41, Haldimand Papers, Public Archives of Canada.

[26]Haldimand Papers, Ainslie Correspondence for 1781, MG 21, B 200-1, pp. 567-75; Governor Sir Frederick Haldimand to the Rt. Hon. Lord Sidney, March 16, 1785, MG 11, Series Q 25, pp. 295-313; Application of Thomas Ainslie April 16, 1786, *op. cit.*, Thomas Steele to Governor Dorchester July 25, 1789, MG 12, T 27/40, Public Archives of Canada.

[27]Manuscript notes of P. G. Ray, Quebec Provincial Archives, Octave

Introduction

The Ainslie "journal" presents a remarkably accurate and precise, although biased, description of the siege of Quebec. In an ordered, methodical manner, the author narrates the principal events of each day from December 1, 1775 through May 7, 1776. Weather conditions, battle strengths of the defenders and the final relief of the garrison are covered in a largely accurate but somehow routine manner. Ainslie's personal biases are usually more lively. He dismisses the French Canadian habitants as little more than cowards and hypocrites. The American invaders, for the most part, are regarded with similar disdain.

From Ainslie's Loyalist perspective, the American Revolution was instigated unjustifiably by malevolent and criminal demagogues—principally from New England.[28] Thus his entry for March 5, 1776, takes note of the patriot observance of the Boston Massacre as an anarchistic celebration honoring illegal resistance against His Majesty's customs officials. Although there are a few grudging notes about his enemies' boldness, Ainslie generally records a skeptical opinion toward Americans as soldiers. One entry made during January, 1776, boasts "we have naught to fear from the natives of America," and later he erroneously predicts that any colonial plans for independence "will end in the ruin of all its abettors."

In the concluding entries of his journal, he rationalizes on the justness of the royalist triumph at Quebec, contrasting an allegedly traitorous and villainous General Montgomery with an effusive description of a gallant and merciful Governor Carleton.[29]

Plessis, *Rapport de l' Archiviste de la province de Quebec*, (Quebec, 1948-9), pp. 3-250. The fact that Ainslie lived a long life is indicated by a letter dated July 4, 1818 from Governor Sherbrooke to Earl Bathurst, Secretary of State for the Colonies, seeking confirmation of the appointment of "Mr. Ainslie" as Clerk of the Crown, MG 11, Series Q 148-2, p. 588, The Public Archives of Canada. Ainslie's second wife, who bore him six children, died in 1787. Judicial Archives of Quebec, Quebec.

[28]See "Transactions in the Frontiers of the Province of Quebec in Summer 1775," from the Thomas Ainslie Journal. Also entry dated May 7, 1776.

[29]Ainslie Journal. See entries for January 17, March 5 and May 7, 1776.

The original manuscript of the Ainslie journal is on deposit at the Houghton Library of Harvard University. Harvard historian Jared Sparks purchased it in London from the manuscript holdings of George Chalmers (1742-1825), a Scottish historian and antiquarian.[30] At least two other handwritten copies of this manuscript exist in British repositories. One dated 1794, and bearing the signature of Governor Carleton's wife Maria, is on deposit in the Rhodes House Library at Oxford University (MSS. Can. r.2.). The other, which dates from the nineteenth century, can be found at the National Maritime Museum in Greenwich, (JOD/66, MS 58/055). One edited version of the Ainslie manuscript was made by Frederic C. Würtele and printed by the Quebec Literary and Historical Society in 1905. Another somewhat similar diary of the siege attributed to a certain J. Danford and covering the period from November 14, 1775, through May 6, 1776, is on deposit at the British Museum. Printed copies of this version appear in William Smith's *History of Canada* and the New York Historical Society *Collections* for 1880.[31] The present edited and annotated version of the original manuscript is published with the acknowledgment and permission of Harvard University.

[30]Thomas Ainslie Journal, MS Sparks 1, Houghton Library, Harvard University. Another, less complete journal, was purchased by Sparks and given to the University. Its author is unknown. See MS Sparks 142, Houghton Library.

[31]Smith, *History of Canada, op. cit.,* II, 84-137; "Journal of the Most Remarkable Occurrences in Quebec from the 14th of November, 1775, to the 7th of May, 1776, By an Officer of the Garrison," New York Historical Society, *Collections,* III (1880), 175-236. The British Museum attributes this work to Danford. Danford apparently based much of his incomplete coverage upon the Ainslie version.

Thos. Ainslie

Journal

of

the most remarkable Occurences

in

the Province of Quebec

from

the Appearance of the Rebels

in September 1775

until their Retreat on the Sixth of May

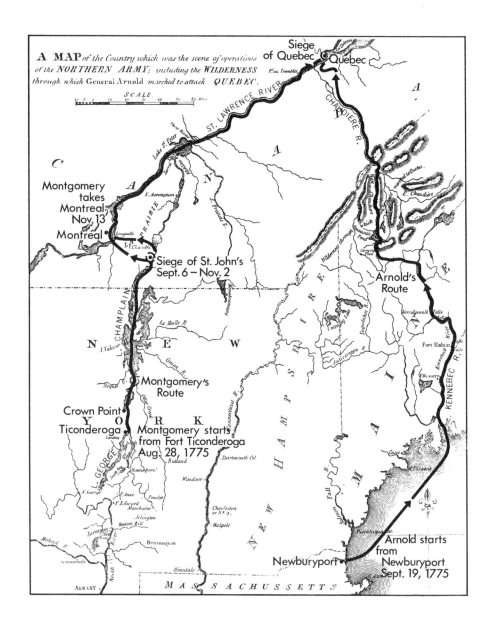

A MAP of the Country which was the scene of operations of the NORTHERN ARMY; including the WILDERNESS through which General Arnold marched to attack QUEBEC.

SCALE

Siege of Quebec

ST. LAWRENCE RIVER

CHAUDIERE R.

Montgomery takes Montreal Nov. 13
Montreal

Siege of St. John's Sept. 6 – Nov. 2

Arnold's Route

L. CHAMPLAIN

Montgomery's Route

Crown Point
Ticonderoga
Montgomery starts from Fort Ticonderoga Aug. 28, 1775

KENNEBEC R.

NEW HAMPSHIRE

MAINE

Newburyport

Arnold starts from Newburyport Sept. 19, 1775

MASSACHUSSETTS

16

Transactions in the Frontiers of the

Province of Quebec in Summer 1775

The N: England Rebels had been long on the watch; they impatiently waited for a pretext to proceed to hostilities. The Lexington affair appear'd to them to be a most favourable crisis. From that day they began to execute their deep laid & long concerted schemes for Independency.

The people of the Colonies in General, at that hour, wou'd have shudder'd at a proposal of that nature; & the cunning N: England Demagogues, knew that that wou'd be an improper time to lay open their intentions to the neighbouring Provinces; but by degrees they led on their unthinking neighbours to take arms against their Mother Country, from the Massachusetts to Georgia the people rose to oppose the Laws; they foresaw they wou'd be able to infatuate the whole Continent, & bring the different Governments under their sway. There lies their ambition—their neighbours may perhaps open their eyes when it will be too late. The first expedition was planned in Connecticut—a man named Allan of that Colony (at the head of a band of adventurers) under the Title of Colonel, stole into the fort at Ticonderoga early in May, and made the Garrison Prisoners, they there (then) proceeded fifteen miles to Crown Point, & took a Sergeant & his command; they sent the whole to Hartford. A few days afterwards they embark'd in batteaus and sail'd down the lake to St. John's, within 21 miles from Montreal & there they surpris'd the Kings sloop; a northerly wind sprung up, they hoisted sail and carried her off to Crown Point.

After these feats there were dayly town meetings, and frequent County Comittees assembled at Albany.[1] At these

17

gatherings of the people, it was held prudent to provide against an attack from Canada; the people were arm'd, and warn'd to be at all times in readiness. Provisions were sent to their friends in Garrison in the forts which Allan had stolen. The result of the consultations of their Grand & petty Congress, the Provincial & County Comittees was not kept secret—it was openly said that the friends of Liberty (for so those who declar'd their firm resolution to oppose the execution of some acts of Parliament, stiled themselves) wou'd penetrate as far into Canada this season as possible. They had robbed the King's mail, and thence stole a return from Gen: Carleton to Gen: Gage, by which they found that the troops in Canada did not amount to seven hundred; on this they prepar'd to invade the Province.[2]

In June the Canadian Peasants began to shew a disposition little to be expected from a conquer'd people who had been treated with so much lenity by Government. The Agents & friends of the Congress had not been idle—by word & by writing they had poison'd their minds—they were brought to believe that the Minister had laid a plan to enslave them, & to make them the instruments of enslaving all the neighbouring Provinces, that they wou'd be continually at War, far removed from their wives and families. Arm'd strangers had appear'd in some of the Parishes below Quebec; they disappear'd suddenly:—nobody knew their business—it was conjectur'd that they came to learn the sentiments of the Country People, & the state of Quebec.[3] Those who knew with what facility the Hunters of N: England can traverse the woods, had apprehensions that the rebels might send parties from their back settlements to harass us near Quebec, in the absence of Gen: Carleton, who was up the country to oppose their entry into Canada by way of St. Johns. Woodsmen may enter this Province by more ways than one—by the Chaudiere and by St. Francis; Rivers taking their rise in the mountains between Canada and N: England; these passes are well known to the back settlers in Massachusetts & in N: Hampshire, there is a third still easier than the two mention'd, by St. Johns river in Nova Scotia and Madawaska River over the carrying place to Kamouraska on the River St. Laurence about an hundred miles below Quebec.

Lieutenant Governor Cramahé[4] took every prudent step to prevent surprise & to stop the progress of Adventurers if they shou'd attempt to come by any of these inlets; he sent a Guard to Sartigan fifty miles south of Quebec on the River Chaudiere; the mouth of St. Francis's river being more than a hundred miles from Quebec, he well knew that they cou'd make no approaches that way, without being discover'd before they reached Three Rivers.

The Agents for the Congress in this Country represented to that body that nothing was to be apprehended from the Canadians in their present temper of mind, that so far from opposing the Continental troops, they would receive them with open arms, nay that perhaps great numbers wou'd join them, for that they appear'd to be thoroughly tinctur'd with the true spirit of Rebellion, thanks to the never ceasing labours of the Malcontents in this Province.

That set of men is composed of a few of the old subjects,[5] & of some Americans from the adjacent Provinces, who have on all occasions taken infinite pains to inflame the minds of the Canadians against Government.

They drew the most hideous pictures of the distresses & miseries, that wou'd be entail'd on the present race, and on their latest posterity if the Quebec Act shou'd take place. From the impressions made by these seditious people, the Canadians look upon the Rebels as their best friends, & are ready to receive them as the asserters of their rights & liberties.

Some of these Grumbletonians are friends to the Constitution but are highly incensed against the Quebec bill.[6]

They see with pain that their malice has contributed to incline the Canadians to throw off their allegiance,—they meant to stir them up to a General application for a repeal of the act, —not to Rebellion.

In the Month of August parties of men in arms were found hovering on our boundaries—at the time we look'd for a visit from the Rebels & were fortifying St. Johns to oppose their progress. We had reconnoitring parties out, one of them was fired at from the bushes, & three Indians were wounded, on which the party made the best of their way back to St. Johns—the Savages swore revenge, a number of them went immediately in pursuit of those who had wounded their brethren.

This party brought in the head of one Baker,[7] it is supposed he led the gang that the Indians went in quest of. The Indians have an inhuman custom of scalping & dismembring the bodies of their dead enemies.

Early in Septr the Rebels appear'd in sight of our fort at St. Johns in three vessels, and about 60 boats. Twelve hundred attempted to land—Capt. Tice[8] at the head of eighty three Indians drove them back, the Capt. was wounded, & four Indians killed—the Rebels had many killed & wounded.

The same Allan who stole into Ticonderoga landed on the Island of Montreal on the 25th of Septr with a party of the Rebels join'd by some Canadians of Chambly, in all about a hundred & fifty, with a design to plunder Montreal.

Gen: Carleton on hearing of their landing, immediately assembled the inhabitants of the City in the Champ de Mars—his excellency shew'd them in a few words the danger which threaten'd the town and the necessity of driving that Banditti back. In an instant the citizens were arm'd, and march'd under Major Campbell's command, to fall on the enemy.[9]

After an hours march they came up with the rebels who were very advantageously posted; however they cou'd not withstand the onset of the brave Montrealists.

They took Allan prisoner and between thirty & forty more, the Rebels had fifteen killed & wounded.[10]

On our side we lost a brave old officer Major Carden an excellent man, justly lamented by the whole Province. We lost Mr. Alex: Patterson, a merchant much beloved by his fellow citizens, & universally esteem'd: we had two more killed & three wounded.

About this time the anarchial method of calling town meetings was adopted in Quebec—in these noisy assemblies the masks of many dropt—their ungarded speeches betray'd principles which policy had made them hide. Reports of Mr. Montgomery's successes were most industriously spread—the enemies of Government continued to watch every favourable opportunity to work on the minds of such of the Old & New subjects as seem'd not yet to be confirmed in their principles—they adress'd the fears of the timid, & spoke to this effect "Our force is small indeed, theirs is now great & it increases daily—let us be prudent —let us remain neuter—let us secure with our effects good treatment from the friends of Liberty, for they will sooner or later take the town; if we attempt to hold out our ruin is unavoidable Why suffer our property to be destroyed. Let us banish all Quixot schemes of defence, & think of terms of surrender."

If report has spoken truth some of the over prudent had drawn out articles of surrender to be laid before the people at one of these meetings—this was in the time that a rumour prevail'd that one Benedict Arnold (the master of a vessel trading from N: England to this place, & from hence to the West Indies with horses)[11] had been detached from the rebel army at Cambridge near Boston with fifteen hundred men, to enter Canada by the rivers of Kennebec & Chaudiere.

The Lieutenant Governor was indefatigable in putting the town in a proper state of defence. The British & the Canadian Militia had been some time embodied. Mr. Cramahé put himself at the head of the British—both corps did Garrison duty.

In October a rebel Colonel named Browne with a body of Provincials and a great number of Canadians cannonaded & took Fort Chambly & made Major Stopford & his garrison seventy prisoners.[12]

On the third of November the Fort at St. Johns was surrendered to Mr. Montgomery, the Garrison was sent prisoners to Hartford in company with the Chambly garrison.

On that day we learnt that a great body of men were not far from Quebec, & that the Canadians living on the banks of the Chaudiere had not attempted to oppose their march. The Lieutenant Governor order'd that all the canoes, shallops, & craft, shou'd be brought off from the opposite shore, & from the Island of Orleans. On the 7th His Majesty's mail was robbed by the rebels near Berthier.

On the 8th a boat from the Hunter sloop of war was fired at from Major Caldwells mill on the Point Levy side, the Captain's brother (Mr. McKenzie, a midshipman) was then on shore amongst the bushes, the boat row'd a little way off. Mr. McKenzie attempted to swim to the boat, but some Indians swam after him & took him prisoner.

On the 9th the Hunter anchor'd off the Mill & batter'd it, a party of the Rebels was lodg'd in it, it is three or four miles above Point Levy.

On the 12th Colonel McLean with a party of his Royal Highland Emigrants, & a few of the Royal Fusiliers arriv'd from Sorrel.[13]

In the night of the 13th Arnold cross'd the River St. Laurence and landed at Wolfe's Cove with the greatest part of his force.

On the 14th a body of men appear'd on the heights of Abraham within 800 yards of the walls of Quebec; they huzza'd thrice —we answer'd them with three chears of defiance, & saluted them with a few cannon loaded with grape & canister shot—they did not wait for a second round.

On the 17th Montreal enter'd into terms of surrender with the rebel General Mr. Montgomery; his people enter'd the town that day.

Some vessels from Montreal with provisions & Brigadier general Prescot[14] with a good many officers & some soldiers on board were obliged to surrender; it appeard impossible to pass some strong batteries which the rebels had erected at the point of Sorel.

Gen: Carleton had order'd all the gunpowder to be destroyed, to the great disappointment of Mr. Montgomery who expected to find a large supply of that essential article which he was much in want of.

On the 19th (a happy day for Quebec) to the unspeakable joy of the friends of Government, & to the utter dismay of the abettors of sedition & rebellion; Gen: Carleton arrived in the Fell, arm'd ship, accompanied by an arm'd schooner—we saw our salvation in his presence.

At this time the Rebels had retir'd to Pointe aux trembles seven leagues above Quebec.

On the 22d a proclamation, most acceptable to the Garrison, was issued by the General commanding all persons contumaciously refusing to enroll their names in the militia lists to assist his Majesties troops in the preservation of the City, against the Rebels who have invaded the Province, & who have appear'd in arms before the town, to quit the town in four days & to withdraw themselves out of the limits of the district of Quebec before the 1st day of December. Thus was our militia purged from all those miscreants who had already taken arms with a design no doubt of turning them against us when a fair opportunity shou'd offer; can a more charitable construction be put on the conduct of those people who bore arms as militia men untill this order appear'd. Cowardice is the mildest term that can be used as a reason why that band forsook their friends—the disgrace attending that step will ever follow them—the consciousness of their pusillanimous behaviour must redden their faces many years hence & make their ofspring blush; whenever Quebec sounds in their ears their shame will appear in their faces; their expulsion much strengthen'd the Garrison—for many people fear'd more the internal enemy than the avowed rebels without the walls, & indeed they were to be dreaded in the day of action—but thanks to the General, their banishment made the minds of the people easy; from that day good things were augur'd by the friends of Government.

When the Rebels appear'd on the plains the Garrison consisted of eleven hundred & twenty six men.

Colonel McLean with his Royal Emigrants & Capt. Owen's fusiliers	200
British Militia	300
Canadian Militia	480
Seamen on shore with Capt. McKenzie	24
Emigrants recruits from N: founland	90
Artificers from Newfounland	32
	1126

An embargo was laid on the ships in harbour, the seamen were order'd on shore—the crews of His Majesties ship the Lizzard & Hunter sloop of war did garrison duty—every townsman fit to bear arms was enrolled in the Militia—they had confidence in the General's abilities & were determin'd to do the duty of good Soldiers.

On the 30th of November the strength of the Garrison was as follows

- 70 Royal Fusiliers.
- 230 Royal Emigrants.
- 22 R: Artillery fire workers &c.
- 330 British Militia.
- 543 Canadian do.
- 400 Seamen.
- 50 Masters & Mates of trading Vessels.
- 35 Marines.
- 120 Artificers.

1800 Men bearing Arms.

The number of souls within the wall computed at 5000— eight months provisions in town. Firewood, hay, oats scarce.[15]

1ST   A foot of snow on the ground, wind S W raw weather with showers of snow. The Hunter sloop of war & the Fell arm'd vessel came down from Richelieu & were laid up. Reported that fifty rebels were lodged at Menuts (a Tavern a mile W of the town) they were soon dislodged by our shot. Clear weather in the evening.

2D   Cloudy wind at S W much floating ice in the river. A man from Lorette was drum'd out of town for having industriously made many dishartning speeches concerning the strength of the Rebels, & for propagating ridiculous stories to intimidate the country people who will swallow the most absurd things when their fears are awaken'd. Arnolds party came thro the woods clad in canvas frocks—the Canadians who first saw them were not a little surprised at their light garb in such cold weather—the report spread that these people were insensible of cold & wore nothing but linnen in the most severe seasons—the French word *toile* (linen) was changed into *tolle* (iron plate) and the rumour then ran that the Bostonois were musket proof, being all cover'd with sheet iron.[16]

The rebels were canton'd from Pointe aux trembles to old Lorette, & small parties of them make frequent excursions toward the town to prevent provisions from being sent in.

The *Habitants* (as the Peasants are called) of the Parish of the Pointe a la caille have prevented a vessel loaded with Provisions from coming to town.

3D   Rain & sleet with N E wind in the morning, S W wind with clear weather in the evening. Many people have heard the report of great guns at a distance. A Canadian has been very industrious in reporting that there are 7000 Russians in the river: he is sent to prison to wait their arrival.[17] The country people say that there are 4500 of the enemy now at P: aux trembles; some came by land, & some by water, & they have many cannon—Mr. Montgomery is at their head.

4TH   It froze hard last night; the weather is clear to day with W wind. The country folks from Beauport still get into town, they say that the Rebels have taken possession of all the houses west of the town, that are not within the reach of our cannon— they further say that a man named Jeremiah Duggan formerly a hair dresser in this place, has the title of Major among the rebels, & that he commands 500 Canadians raised at Chambly.[18]

If the rebel General gives commissions to such men his army will not be formidable.

5TH   In the night Jere: Duggan headed a party to disarm the inhabitants of the suburbs of St. Roc—it is more than probable he was invited to pay them a visit by those who wanted an excuse for laying down their arms. They cou'd have alarm'd the Garrison with ease, but they lay snug. As they have been obliged to give their Paroles not to carry arms, they are going into the Country. A Soldier of the British Militia was tried by a court Martial on a charge of a Sergeant for refusing to do duty. Acquitted. Tis said that the Rebels are at work behind a house within a mile of the walls, intending to raise a battery there—we sent several shot thro the house.

Our situation will not admit of scouting parties, we must depend on chance for information of the enemies motions.

6TH   Wind W S W cloudy & cold.

A woman of St. Roc gave information at Palace Gate that some of the Rebels lay drunk at her house, & that a small party cou'd take them without risk. This woman (of ill fame) was perhaps sent to get a few men into the rebels clutches—she was told to let them know that they wou'd be well treated if they came in; a little while after a man calling himself a cockney surrender'd himself at Palace Gate—at dusk three more came in. The Riflemen hid themselves behind houses walls rocks fences &c watching for a shot, wherever a sentry shew'd his head over the walls they fir'd, directed by their smoke we return'd their fire, there was nobody hurt on our side.

7TH   Wind at E cloudy: "the prisoners say Mr. Montgomery is at Holland house, two miles S W of St Johns gate.[19] Detachments are quarter'd in Charlebourg, Beauport, and the adjacent parishes: they are Two Thousand strong including the Canadians.

"Mr. Montgomery intends to open batteries to canonade & bombard us & in the height of our distress & terror the rebels are to storm the town.

"One of the Prisoners was formerly in the Kings service at the Siege of this place: he was a Sergeant with the Rebels; he said one day in the hearing of an Officer that it wou'd not be an easy matter to get over the walls of Quebec. You rascal, said he, do you mean to dishearten the men. This he gives as one reason for his hastening his departure, for he had long intended to join us, as he cou'd not think of drawing his sword against his country-men. He was born in Ireland; no Gentleman he says wou'd be led by such Officers—they are for the greatest part low Mechanics, especially those from New England.

8TH   There fell six inches of snow last night, the wind is S W to day freezing clear weather. Skulking Riflemen watching to fire on those who appear on the ramparts—We saw a man drop; we pop at all those who come within musket shot knowing their intention is to kill any single person walking on the ramparts—this is the American way of making war. The indignation of our Militia is raised against these fellows who call themselves soldiers —they are worse than Savages, they will ever be held in contempt with men of courage. Lie in wait to shoot a sentry! a deed worthy of Yanky men of war.

We saw many people go out & in at Menuts. A cannon ball took off the head of a horse which stood at the door & shatterd the Cariole [sleigh] in which he was tackled in a thousand pieces.

9TH   Wind at W soft & pleasant. Various reports concerning the enemy: from what the deserters have said, confirm'd by some country people, we imagine there are about 1500 men under Mr. Montgomery. The small pox does havock among them—there are 200 now in hospitals, tis a deadly infection in Yanky veins. We have long had that disorder in town.

10TH   Cloudy & very cold wind at N E. About two oclock this morning 28 small shells of 5-2 In: were thrown into Town;

one went thro the roof of a house but did no further damage. At day light we discover'd fascines in form of a battery about 800 yds S W of Port St. Johns.

The tops of the houses in the suburbs near the gate hinder'd our view of the enemies works, we therefore set fire to these houses & batter'd down their gable ends. We kept up a constant fire on their works from different parts.

11TH   High wind at S W with heavy rain. 43 shells were thrown into Town last night.

Before they gave us a sample of their savoir faire in the bombarding way, the towns people had conceived that every shell wou'd inevitably kill a dozen or two of people, & knock down some two or three houses; some were in fears about their tenements, but the greatest part were occupied about the safety of their persons: they had anticipated much evil: but after they saw that their bombettes as they called them, did no harm, women and children walked the streets laughing at their former fears. They kept up a constant poping at our sentries in the night: wherever a noise was heard, or a light shewn, balls flew thick in that direction.

About midday the wind veer'd suddenly to N W, it blew a perfect hurricane—it froze so hard that in half an hour the streets & ramparts were cover'd with ice.

12TH   Wind at W freezing hard. 40 shells were thrown into town in the night—firing as usual on our sentries we return'd shot for shot. One man was kill'd on the ramparts to day.

13TH   Fine soft weather, wind at W—three shells only were thrown into town last night—the roofs of two houses were damaged—some days ago a report prevail'd that the rebels intended to erect a battery on the Point Levy side, to play on the town from that quarter.

We saw some people about the ferrymans house on the opposite beach, we sent a 9 lb shot thro the house, & out scrambled a number of men who never look'd behind them until they reached the summit of the hill: there they stood and dis-

charg'd their muskets. The distance from the Kings wharf to high water mark on the other side is between 11 & 1200 yards.
Rifle parties in St. Roc to day—some of them got into the Cupulo in the Intendant Palace there, & fired into the Town.[20] The barrack yard, & a great part of the ramparts are open to people there placed; a nine pounder soon forced them to quit that station. It is probable that we killed & wounded a good many to day, as they appear'd in numbers in the streets of St. Roc; we saw bodies put into sleighs & carried off. We saw men at work at the fascines, which we discover'd on the heights on the 10th. We sent many balls among them, & threw some shells into their works, yet with our glasses we cannot perceive we have done much damage.

14TH   There was not a shell thrown by the enemy last night— there fell a little snow—louring weather, wind at W. At midday the rebels opened a battery of five Guns on the heights, they are six, nine, & twelve pounders.
We were not slack in returning 18 lb, 24 lb & 32 lb shot— with pleasure we saw our balls pierce their works. Their shot had no more effect upon our walls, than pease wou'd have against a plank.[21]

15TH   Wind at E mild. A few shells were thrown in the last night—they fire from their battery to day—we answer. A great pillar of smoak arose in an instant in their works—we believe something has blown up. About nine in the morning we saw a man beating a drum follow'd by two dressed in blanket coats— one carried a handkerchief or some such thing on a stick—we permitted them to approach near the walls—they desired to speak with the General—they were told they wou'd not be admitted, nor wou'd any letter or message be receiv'd from them—they were ordered to march off—they said, "then let the General be answerable for all consequences" & away they went.
Towards evening they fired from their battery—they threw no shells at night—we have almost destroyed their works.

16TH   A fine mild day—wind S W. no shells thrown last night —in the afternoon they fired on the town from three guns & threw some small shells. We have undoubtedly dismounted some of their guns.

The riflemen firing from garret windows in St. Roc wounded three men on the ramparts. In the night we threw some shells into St. Roc.

At four o clock in the morning the sentry behind the Artillery barracks left his post & alarm'd Palace Gate guard with a report that 600 men were marching up to the walls.

The drums beat to arms, the great Bell of the Cathedral rang the alarm—every man ran arm'd to his post, & there the Garrison remained waiting the attack, but no enemy appear'd. It blew excessively hard, with a heavy fall of snow.

17TH   Wind at E. snowy stormy dark cold weather—nothing extraordinary.

18TH   Snowy mild day wind at S. Some shells thrown into town to day—we sent some into St. Roc. We do not see many people this morning—they have carried away their Guns, or have drawn them behind the shatter'd embrasures. We had a man shot thro the head by a ball from a Garret in St. Roc. Wou'd to God that the suburbs were reduced to ashes, it only serves as a cover from which our enemies teaze us continually.

19TH   Mild snowy weather, wind at S. Some firing on our sentries last night by people concealed in St. Johns suburbs. We threw shells & carcasses into St. Roc, & burnt four houses there. Cold afternoon.

20TH   Very cold, wind at W. nothing in the night remarkable. If this weather shall continue, Mr. Montgomery would find it difficult to eat his Christmas dinner in Quebec. A threat is put into his mouth—it is reported that he swore—"he wou'd dine in Quebec or in Hell on Christmas." We are determined he shall not dine in town & be his own master. From his General character we are apt to think that these words are not his.

The weather is very severe indeed, no man after having been exposed to the air but ten minutes, cou'd handle his arms to do execution. Ones senses are benumb'd. If ever they attack us it will be in mild weather.

The quantity of ice & snow now heap'd up in the places we have reckoned the weakest, are (thanks to the Climate) exceeding strong.

One of our townsmen who is a prisoner with the Rebels, has found means it is said, to convey a letter into town to day, which marks—"that their Canadian aids leave them very fast & that their own people are quite tir'd of the expedition."

On our side we gather spirits every day, if one may draw conclusions from appearances, we'll make a stout defence.

21ST   Clear weather, excessively cold, wind W N W, nothing remarkable.

22D   The cold continues to be excessive wind W S W. Colonel Caldwells clerk who has been a prisoner with the rebels for some days got away, & came by way of Wolfes Cove into Pres de Ville at 10 o'clock at night.

23D   In the morning cold—mild at noon. Colonel Caldwells clerk reports "that the rebels intend to storm the town to night. Their leader Mr. Montgomery has hitherto found it impossible to engage his followers to undertake a step so desperate. He has promis'd to the amount of 200£ in plunder to every man. The Europeans say the Americans shou'd first mount the walls, but they are not covetous of that honour—they have 500 scaling ladders made in a very clumsy manner."

Can these men pretend that there is a possibility of approaching our walls loaden with ladders, sinking to the middle every step in snow!

Where shall we be then? shall we be looking on cross arm'd?

It will be a fatal attempt for them, they will never scale the walls.

A deserter came with the Clerk, they say the enemy is about 2000; they are sickly—the dread of the small pox kills many of the poor creatures.

A man was shot to day (from a garret window in St Roc) on the two gun battery.

24TH   Mild weather, cloudy, wind N E—nothing remarkable happen'd last night. In consequence of Mr. Wolfes (the Clerk) information, above a thousand men were ready to oppose the Rebels in case of an attack; the rest of the Garrison lay in their cloaths with their arms and accoutrements lying by them.

A deserter from the Rebels (a discharg'd man from the 28th) came running towards St Johns gate—he fir'd his musket into the air & club'd it—he called to be let in—the gate being block'd up, he was drawn in by ropes.

He reported that the attack was put off on account of Mr. Wolfe's escape, but he say they will surely attempt the town to night if his escape does not prevent them.

Mr. Montgomery had just stept out of the Cariole which was knock'd to pieces by a cannon shot at Menuts door on the 8th.[22]

25TH   Every thing was remarkably quiet last night—we saw many lights all around us, which we took for signals.

The whole Garrison almost was under arms expecting & ardently wishing for the long threatn'd attack.

The weather is mild, wind at S W.

"The rebels pay the Habitants with paper: these pusillanimous avaricious caitifs are well served—they will find it of very little service in the month of May next."

Gen: Carleton sleeps in his cloaths in the Recollets, & so do all the men & officers off duty.[23]

26TH   This is no wall scaling weather—the night was clear & inconceivably cold—it is employment enough to preserve ones nose. The wind is at N W piercingly keen—nothing extraordinary.

27TH   Hazy cloudy weather last night, snow this morning with the wind at W N W.

28TH   All was quiet last night, the weather clear and mild. The wind is S W to day.

29TH   Clear fine weather all the night, no alarm, wind W N W—we get no intelligence. We see the rebels crossing the streets in St Roc arm'd; some are cloth'd in red. They take care to shew themselves out of musket reach, & where no guns bear.

30TH   The wind is Easterly & mild. Last night a deserter (an intelligent fellow, an Irishman) came in from the rebels.

He reports that "they are three thousand strong, having been reinforced from Montreal; that they have been cloath'd lately; they have plenty of provisions. The Habitants supply them with every thing for wch they are paid in hard money—they refuse to take the Congress bills until the Town falls, they'll then accept of them. The small pox still rages among them, they have got a supply of shells from Montreal.

"Last Wednesday evening the whole army was under arms at head quarters in order to march to the attack of the Town. Mr. Montgomery inform'd them that the time was unfavourable, but that he wou'd soon lead them to an easy & glorious conquest. He thank'd them for the zeal & spirit they had shewn & so dismiss'd them."

This deserter said that "the Americans express'd much impatience to be led to the attack, but his opinion is that they will be very backward on seeing the fire of our great guns. All the Europeans wish to be at home they do not pretend to like the intended attack."

"We shall certainly be attack'd the first dark night."

Twenty eight shells were thrown into Town; they did no hurt: a third part of them did not burst.

31ST   It snow'd all the night, it was very dark, the wind was strong at N E.

About 4 o clock in the Morning Capt: Malcom Fraser of the Royal Emigrants being on his rounds, saw many flashes of fire without hearing any reports; the sentries inform'd him that they had perceived them for some time on the heights of Abraham, the sentinels between Port Louis & Cape Diamond had seen fix'd lights like lamps in a street—these appearances being very uncommon & the night favouring the designs of the enemy, Capt:

Fraser order'd the Guards and Pickets on the ramparts to stand to their arms. The drums beat, the bells rang the alarm, & in a few minutes the whole Garrison was under arms—even old men of seventy were forward to oppose the attackers.

Two Rockets sent by the enemy from the foot of Cape Diamond were immediately followed by a heavy & hot fire from a body of men posted behind a rising ground within eighty yards of the wall, at Cape Diamond, the flashes from their muskets made their heads visible—their bodies were cover'd: we briskly return'd the fire directed by theirs—at this moment a body of men suppos'd to be Canadians appear'd in St Johns suburbs,—& the enemy threw shells into town from St Roc.

Colonel Caldwell conducted a detachment of the British Militia to reinforce Cape Diamond. It was said by some of the deserters that Mr. Montgomery believ'd it was the weakest place where an escalade cou'd be easily effected; the Colonel having posted his men under proper officers, return'd to the Corps de reserve on the Parade to wait the Generals orders. The Rockets were the signal; when Arnold saw them he pushed on from St Rocs to attack our works at Saut au Matelot with nine hundred pick'd men, Mr. Montgomery advanced towards the works at Pres de Ville with seven hundred of his best soldiers.[24]

Arnolds party was obliged to pass close under the pickets behind the Hotel Dieu & Montcalms house, where they were exposed to a dreadful fire of small arms which the Sailors pour'd down on them, as they passed. Arnold was here wounded in the leg & carried off:—his men proceeded, forced our guard, & got possession of our battery at Saut au Matelot.

They penetrated about two hundred yards further to a barrier where we made a stand—a brisk firing began on both sides—the rebels fired under cover; we only saw those who ventur'd to run from one house to another, in that way they advanc'd. Gen: Carleton attentive to the most minute manoeuvre of the enemy, skilled in military matters, saw in a moment & instantaneously improv'd the advantage the rebels had given over them. He sent Capt. Laws with sixty men out of Palace gate to attack them in rear, & Capt: McDougal of the R: Emigrants was dispatched a little while after to support them with 60 more.

WITHSTANDING THE ATTACK OF ARNOLD'S MEN AT THE SECOND BARRIER

Captn. Laws advanced too far; impatient to be among them he got before his men; he commanded a group of the Rebels to surrender—seeing him unattended they disarm'd him. Capt. McDougal came up with the first party who were in possession of the battery, they join'd him & releas'd Capt. Laws.[25]

As the Gen: had plann'd they were effectually hem'd in—to advance they dared not,—retreat they cou'd not—they laid down their arms & called for Quarter.

Captns. Laws & McDougal acquir'd much honour by their conduct & bravery on this occasion. At Pres de Ville the sentries had seen the flashes very early, the guard was posted expecting the attack.

Capt. Barnsfair (master of a Merchantman) had charge of the battery that morning: he had his men early at Quarters, they stood by the guns with lighted matches. A strict look out was kept; men were seen approaching—a band advances within fifty yards of our guns—there they stood as if in consultation. In a little while they sprung forward—Capt. Barnsfair called *Fire.* Shrieks & groans followed the discharge. Our musketry & guns continued to sweep the avenue leading to the battery for some minutes—when the smoke clear'd away there was not a soul to be seen. Much has been said in commendation of Mr. Coffin's cool behaviour; his example at Pres de Ville had a noble effect on his fellow soldiers, they behav'd with the greatest spirit.

Those who were engaged at the barrier, were reinforc'd by two detachments from the Parade.

Major Nairne of the R Emigrants led the first, he & Mesr's Dembourges of the same corps attracted the notice of every body by their gallant behaviour.[26]

The Rebels had got possession of a house which commanded Lymburne's battery & one of the principal streets; they mounted ladders & intrepidly forced their way by the windows, & drove the Rebels out at the door.

Every power of Col: McLean was exerted on this occasion, he had his eye every where to prevent the progress of the attackers; his activity gave life to all who saw him—he follow'd the Gens: orders with military judgment.

Col: Caldwell by his example made the British Militia

emulous to appear wherever danger made their presence most necessary.

The seamen were under the strictest discipline. Col: Hamilton & Major McKenzie led on the brave fellows, who behaved as they do on all occasions, like British Tars.

The handful of R. Fusiliers commanded by Capt. Owen distinguished themselves—& the R: Emigrants behav'd like Veterans.

The Canadian militia shew'd no kind of backwardness,—a few of them stood to the last at a little breastwork near the battery at Saut au Matelot; when they were in the greatest danger of being surrounded, they retreated to the barrier.

The Flower of the rebel army fell into our hands. We have reason to think that many of Arnold's party were killed in advancing, & many killed & wounded in endeavouring to get back. Our fire from the Pickets gall'd them exceedingly.

We made prisoners—

1	Lieut Colonel
2	Majors
8	Captains
15	Lieutenants
1	Adjutant
1	Quarter Master
4	Volunteers
350	Private
44	Officers & Soldiers wounded
426	Taken

The prisoners think that Mr. Montgomery's party has not behav'd with that spirit which Arnolds shew'd—they say that if they had advanced like men, our force wou'd have been divided, & the two bodies wou'd have driven us before them, until they got us between two fires.

They little know the situation at Pres de Ville who talk thus: but allow for a moment that they had carried the Lower Town, they wou'd have been but little advanc'd towards getting possession of the upper town, from whence we can burn the houses below us at any time. Shells wou'd soon have reduced it to a heap of rubbish.

The prisoners had slips of Paper pin'd to their hats with these words

Liberty or Death

We had kill'd Capt. Anderson formerly a Lt in the Navy, four private men; one man dangerously wounded & thirteen slightly. Dealer, a brave Militia gunner, was shot thro the Jaw.[27]

We took their bomb battery at St Roc, we found there—

Two Royals
Three Cohorns[28]
And two brass three pounders, with a quantity of small shells.

The whole affair was over by eight in the morning & all the Prisoners were securely lodged.

1ST   Last night there fell a great quantity of snow. The whole Garrison lay on their arms, every thing remain'd quiet—thirteen dead bodies were found very near our work at Pres de Ville, they were brought to town.

Two deserters came in to day; on their report that Mr. Montgomery is missing the dead bodies were shewn to the Prisoners. They pointed out their General's, his aid de Camps Mr McPherson's, & a Capt. Cheeseman's.[29]

Mr. Meigs stiled Major among the prisoners obtain'd liberty to go to head quarters accompanied by Monsieur Lanaudiere the Generals Aid de Camp, to demand the baggage of these people.[30]

Mr. Lanaudiere saw by a great number of the Canaille assembled at the end of St Roc, that it wou'd be most prudent for him to return to Town: it is more than probable that the crew he there saw wou'd have detain'd him—these people impatiently waited a messenger from the town to anounce the opening of the gates. It was reported before daylight that the Lower town was in Mr. Montgomerie's possession; this acceptable piece of news, brought all the blackguards of the adjacent Parishes to St Roc to wait the surrender of the upper town, & they firmly believ'd that Major Meigs was the messenger.

These rascals had not the courage to pass the Pickets in the way to Saut au Matelot, & they were afraid to pass on the ice for fear of our great guns—there they lay until night convinc'd them that their friends had catch'd a Tartar.

A genteel coffin is order'd by the Lt: Governor for the interment of Mr. Montgomery: those who knew him formerly in this place, sincerely lament his late infatuation, they say he was a genteel man, and an agreeable companion.

2D   All the last night we kept up an incessant fire on St Roc, & threw many shells into its suburbs.

A volunteer in the Rebel army came over from Beauport to Saut au Matelot on the ice, he imagin'd that the officer of that guard was willing to divert himself, when he told him that he was prisoner. He left Beauport with a design to join Arnolds party.

Mr. Meigs obtain'd permission to go to the head quarters

of the enemy on his parole to return in three days, he is to demand the Prisoners baggage.

3D   A soft cloudy day. Shot & shells fired into St Roc. The Prisoners dreading the small pox and apprehensive of taking the infection the natural way have requested to be inoculated—their petition is granted, & they are preparing for that operation.[31]

4TH   Nothing remarkable happen'd last night: the wind is at S W to day hazy drizzling weather. Capt. Anderson's body was interr'd with all the honours of War. Mr. Montgomery's was privately buried at night.

5TH   Thawing, wind S W—it sleeted all the last night; this weather is very uncommon at this season.
      We are making additions to the works at Saut au Matelot. Firing heard towards St Foix.
      Mr. Meigs return'd with part of the baggage

6TH   Wind N W freezing; the cold increases as the Sun rises.

7TH   The wind is at W very cold. Some of the St Roc people who had formerly served in the Militia, who tamely suffer'd Duggan to take away their arms, & who had left their habitations to herd with the ill affected Canadians in the Country were found skulking in the suburbs to day: they are in confinement on suspicion of having been aiding & assisting to the Rebels.
      The day after the attack, it was current in the country that we had been beat out of the Lower town with a loss of six hundred killed & that Mr. Montgomery had lost but 15 men. Ninety four of the prisoners, all Europeans they say, have petitioned for leave to enlist in Col: McLeans Corps.

8TH   Wind at N E cloudy raw weather blowing hard. The 94 petitioners took the oaths, they swore to serve His Majesty faithfully until the first of June next: Their engagements with the congress ended the last day of December. Before the oaths were tender'd to them, they were told to consider well of the matter:

they unanimously said, that they wished to atone for their past error by serving the King faithfully.

Some people who pretend to understand the Policy of those who have imbibed N: England principles, say that their oaths will not bind them, for they are in their hearts convinc'd that it is lawful for them to use every means to obtain their liberty: & they see no way left but to practice on the good & unsuspicious tempers of the folks from the Old Country—Many wagers were laid that the greatest part of them will take the very first opportunity to desert. Others say that as they are represented to be a praying, Psalm singing, devout people, their just sense of religion makes their bare word as sacred as their oath. Time will try if the Ante Yankites conjectures are well founded.

9TH   There fell a great quantity of snow before morning, the wind is at N E & it blows still, the air is mild.

10TH   Wind W N W blowing very hard, snowing & intensely cold.

The sentries observed many flashes of fire towards St Foix & near the General Hospital. The guards were on that account very watchful, an attack being apprehended. This morning it is difficult to pass in the streets for the drifted snow—in the narrow lanes some were obliged to dig their way out of their houses.

11TH   Wind W by N very cold & very clear: it drifted so in the afternoon so as to choak the streets. Rockets were play'd off last night at St Foix, Beauport, at the General Hospital, & W end of St Roc. A few muskets were fir'd on our sentries overlooking St Roc, they were answer'd by an 18 lb loaded with grape & canister shot.

The men who came in the day after the attack were conducted to Pt: Levy in a canoe by two Recollets; if they have reported the truth the Rebels know the strength of the Garrison & the good condition of our works.

12TH   Wind S W nothing remarkable—a drifting afternoon.

13TH   The weather was very bad the last night. This morning Palace gate was opend for those who were in want of wood. An arm'd body was sent to cover the workers, many people supplied themselves plentifully—there is much fire wood in St Roc; about nine o clock at night many short lived blazes were seen at the W end of St Roc.

14TH   Wind at W excessively cold. There appears something like a battery at the S end of the General Hospital.

15TH   Last night it froze very hard—to day we have a high S W wind intollerably cold with much drift.
    A report is spread in Town (it can't be traced) that the inhabitants of Montreal have refus'd to comply with an oppressive order issued by their new Masters; & that the Canadians thereabout have refus'd to follow Mr. Wooster (the rebel General) to Quebec.[32]
    The death of Mr. Montgomery has, in seeming, cool'd the courage of the Habitants.

16TH   Keen frost last night.
    A noise like that of men at work with axes was heard in St Rock about the Intendants palace.
    The Archives were brought in from the vaults of that building to day.

17TH   A girl of the town who had been kept in confinement by the Rebels on suspicion of having convey'd intelligence to us, found means to escape them to day.
    She says that "Two Hundred of them have deserted since their defeat, & that they talk of another attack with four thousand Men."
    If we consider the number killed and taken, there cannot be above 800 of the rebels remaining. If they depend on the Canadians for aid, they trust a very rotten support; we within the walls wou'd laugh at an army of 10,000 habitants. We have nought to fear from the natives of America, it is the Euro-

peans who have enter'd into the service of the Congress who give the Colonists what strength they have.[33]

This Girl spoke with the men whom the Recollets landed on the 11th at P Levy; the rebels did not relish their report. the wind is N E it snows & is cold.

18TH   Wind S W fine weather but cold.

The guns were fir'd in honour of Her Majesty.

A mill wrought by horses was set a going to day; it makes fine flower in great quantity.

19TH   Cold clear Easterly wind. Five sleighs loaden with baggage for the Prisoners came to Palace Gate to day escorted by an officer carrying a flag of truce, as they call a handkerchief fix'd to a stick, this is waved by the bearer as a signal that he approaches the walls with no hostile intention; he brought a little money for the Prisoners.

About nine at night a fire broke out in St Roc—whether it took by accident, or was kindled by the rebels we know not.

20TH   Wind S W with falls of soft snow.

We fir'd at their guard house at the W end of St Roc & threw a good many shells in that direction—it is close under a rocky precipice; we can see a part of its roof & a bit of the gable end—some of our shot found a way thro it.

Six houses were burnt in St Roc in the night—they began to blaze about ten o clock; there is no doubt now who burns them.

21ST   Mild weather with snow, wind at S W.

Last night three of Col. McLean's new recruits (from the prisoners) deserted, they will no doubt make a true report to the Rebel chief which will give him very little desire to attempt Quebec.

About ten this morning a small sloop lying within four hundred yards of Palace gate was seen in flames, tho' many small craft lay near her no farther damage was done.

Six or eight sentries have this place in view but these night workers crawl on hands & feet in the dark, strike a light in the hold, set fire to a slow match communicating with combustibles, creep away again, & are out of reach before the fire blazes. A great quantity of fire wood was got in from St Roc to day.

22D   Wind at N E not cold, but windy cloudy & drifty. About two o clock this morning more houses were set on fire in St Roc.

A great quantity of rum & molasses are lying in Mr. Drummonds distillery without palace gate.

It is thought prudent to bring it into town, as the wind may carry the fire that way.

23D   S W wind & mild weather.—Palace gate open.

A body of men with a brass three pounder, cover'd the wooding party. Great quantities were got in to day.

About nine at night some houses in the W end of St Roc were set on fire, fourteen were consum'd before morning. The night was still & gloomy, the snow loaded clouds hung low, from them an orange tinge was reflected, & the snow as far as the flames gave light, was of a redish yellow. The adjacent country seem'd cover'd with a pitchy fire, & the villages were just perceptible in a dismal gloom.

The scene was pleasingly awful, nothing was heard but the crakling of burning beams, & a hollow roaring of fierce flames. To borrow Miltons expression "darkness & visible" in every street & in every narrow alley in Town.

If the rebels did not despair of taking the city wou'd they burn the suburbs? it has been their shelter & cover for their riflemen.

The Gen: wou'd have burnt both St. John & St. Roc long ago, but in commiseration of the poor proprietors he let the houses stand.

24TH   A fine mild day, wind at S W.

A guard of eighteen men to mount at retreat beating every evening outside of Palace gate to prevent the Rebels from stealing towards the Canotrie.[34]

Some houses towards the N W extremity of St Roc were burnt at night.

25TH.   Wind S W mild & clear. A strong party was sent out with a brass six pounder on wheels to cover the wood cutters.

Gen: Carleton attended by Col: McLean advanced within musket shot of the enemies guard house: We do not know what his Excellencies intention was, but if the road had been so as the six pounder cou'd have been brought up, we imagine that a good account wou'd have been given of their advanc'd guard.

A little while afterwards we saw three small bodies of men advancing towards St Roc from Menuts & the General Hospital.

For some days past we have seen great numbers of sleighs passing from Beauport, Orleans &cc towards the General Hospital, perhaps with provisions for the Rebels.

In the fall a vessel loaden with Rum was forc'd on shore on Orleans by stress of weather, perhaps they are carrying her cargo to their Magazines.

They do not come so near the Town as they were wont to do before a shot knock'd a sleigh topsy turvy.

26TH   Easterly wind, heavy sky, a little snow.

It is rumour'd to day that one Dumont "who left the town to secure himself in the Country, was plunder'd at Charlebourg, it is not said whether by Canadian or N England rebels: & they add that one Larche who forsook his house in St Roc was kill'd, defending his property at Beauport."

27TH   Wind S W cold weather. The brass six pounder is mounted on runners, & was sent out to day to cover a wooding party.

28TH   Nothing remarkable—wind S W excessively cold.

29TH   Wind W clear weather intensely cold: it freezes as the Canadians say, *a pierre fendre* [to split a stone].

If this weather shall continue but a few day's the River will be froze up, an event that wou'd double the duty of the Garrison

—guards must in that case be posted in many parts of the Lower Town, which are open to the beach.

30TH   The cold continues, the sky o'ercast, the wind is easterly. P.M; the wind increases.

It blows very hard & snows this evening, at ten the Rebels fir'd some houses in St. Roc: these fire bearers take care to keep at a good distance from our outside sentries.

31ST   Wind E dark soft weather, drizling. Four men on snow shoes came thro' the fields towards St. Roc; we took them for deserters coming in—they stop'd suddenly & discharg'd their muskets but at too great a distance to hurt our working party. Our great guns were fir'd at them, on perceiving the smoak they drop'd down on the snow & got up again after the balls had pass'd over, & made the best of their way back from whence they came.

About nine at night they set fire to some houses which remain'd standing at the N W end of St. Roc. The blaze gave light in every corner of the town.

1ST   Wind at S W blowing drifty & cold, we had a working party outside to day, some shots were fir'd at them from behind fences but at too great distance to do any hurt.

An English woman obtain'd leave of the Gen: to join her husband in the country. She cou'd not pass the guard at the W End of St Roc, the people on duty there made her return; she says they were all Canadians.

2D   Wind W nothing remarkable, a house in St Roc burnt.

3D   Wind S W clear sunshine excessively cold—a wooding party out—cover'd—firing from behind old walls on our men at work. A shell from the Town soon made their skulking place deserted.

In the night our out sentries discover'd a small body cautiously stealing forward, shoudering the wall under the artillery barracks: the guard was alarm'd: but their eagerness to surround them made them uncautious, & they were discoverd. the enemy fled precipitately.

We conjecture that they intended to pass on to the canotrie & set fire to the houses in that quarter: the wind favour'd such an intention.

4TH   Wind at W exceeding cold. If the cold continues to this degree the River will inevitably be froze over the next low Tides.

From the small quantity of ice now floating we think that it is taken opposite the Chaudiere six miles above the Town.

5TH   Wind W cloudy weather, the cold is not so severe as it was yesterday—while the wind blows the river will not freeze.

6TH   W wind blowing drifting day, & cold. In the night three of the converted rebels deserted; they let themselves drop over the wall behind the artillery barracks, where the snow was drifted very high, from thence they slid 30 or 40 foot down a steep, cover'd over with snow, into the street at St Roc.

If the sentry who was posted not more than thirty yards from the spot, had done his duty, they cou'd not have escap'd, three of the same set were confin'd for hinting an intention to follow them.

7TH   Wind at S W clear & cold. Last night three houses were burnt in St Johns suburbs, there is a quantity of cord wood there & some hay, the rebels know we are in want of both.

A 24 pounder commands the main street, seven people have been seen at the upper end of it, & five in their old battery to day.

8TH   A soft clear morning. there remains but very little wood in St Roc—we have cut down the pickets equal with the snow, when that melts 2 or 3 feet we'll find a second crop.

Three men bending their course over the ice from Orleans towards the town were overtaken by 18 from Beauport; they all return'd together.

Capt Nairne acting as Major of the British Militia guarded St. Johns suburbs with 30 men last night.

9TH   A heavy wind at N E with thick snow—before the morning the storm increas'd to a perfect hurricane, it was impossible to face the weather but for a minute.

A sailor is missing, it is very probable he will be found buried under the snow next spring, in some places it is drifted 20 foot high; if he attempted to desert, he must have perish'd inevitably.

10TH   Wind still at N E & but little moderate, the streets are impassible in many places but on snow shoes. The first stories of many houses are under the snow, the windows of the second story serve as doors, by which to pass into the streets.

About eight in the evening the wind fell suddenly & the snow abated.

11TH   A man (the new recruits call'd him Capt: Felton) carrying a stick with a napkin fix'd to it, was permitted to advance close to the walls facing St Roc. He said that he had letters for Governor Carleton from Mr. Abbot & Mr. Schaulch of the R Artillery.[35] A message was sent to the General—Colonel McLean return'd & inform'd the man that his Excellencies pleasure was, that he immediately go back from whence he came— that no message, nor shou'd any letters be receiv'd thro the Channel of the Rebels—he added *never let a like attempt be made*. The man walk'd off.

12TH   Wind S W a fine moderate day, strong working parties employ'd to clear the ditch & ramparts of snow. In some places the snow is so drifted as to render it very easy to walk out at an embrasure into the ditch, & many of the guns are deeply buried in this drift altho their muzzles are at least 30 foot from the bottom of the ditch.

13TH   A fine moderate day. All the officers & men off duty employ'd to clear the ramparts & ditch.

Above a hundred of the prisoners have been sent sick to the Hospital within these few days past.

14TH   Wind at S W with fine weather—above eighty loaded sleighs have gone from different quarters to Menuts. With our glasses we see two field pieces at his door—there is a crowd of people always about his house, & many pass & repass between that & the Gen: Hospital.

If they have been transacting any extraordinary business to day we have disturb'd them not a little with our shot.

After we had kept up a hot fire for some time, the old signal a clout on a stick was seen waving in an advancing Cariole— we seem'd to take no kind of notice of this flag as they call it, we still aim'd at our mark, & the flagman still advanc'd, he pass'd their guard house at the end of St Roc; at last he stop'd his Cariole, stood up, & wav'd his signal: we still fir'd at Menuts. We suppose that he (just at that instant) recollected the answer given to Mr. Felton on the 11th—he turn'd his horse's head, & trotted back.

He saw that we understood their finesse. We think it was a piece of their soldiership, to engage us to desist from firing until they cou'd remove somebody or somethings of consequence, find-

49

ing the house too hot for them. Three of the Emigrants are missing to day, one of them is a new recruit.

We saw about a hundred men, at a house half a mile or more West of the end of St. Johns suburbs, to the left of the old battery—we imagine there is something in agitation among them, they have been bustling about during the last 24 hours.

We heard three huzza's from about the General Hospital last night; we conjecture that they have had a reinforcement from Montreal or perhaps the promise of a strong reinforcement may have raised their drooping spirits.

If they wait for a reinforcement by way of lake George and Lake Champlain their courage will cool. If they make a second attack they will repent their rashness—but we'll see.

15TH   A dark louring morning with a cold N E wind.

About 11 o clock last night fire broke out on both sides of the main street in St Johns Suburbs—six houses were consum'd —no person had been seen there in the evening. We fir'd some random shot among the houses.

16TH   Westerly wind with fine mild weather. A strong party on fatigue clearing away the snow in the ditch. Even after this day's work, ladders of 14 feet will reach from the top of the snow bank in the ditch, at Cape Diamond to the embrasures in many places.

Between 9 & 10 oclock last night the rebels attempted to set fire to two vessels lying at the wharf at St Roc, & to a house in St Johns suburbs—neither of them burn'd. In the evening a 12 pound shot fell in St Louis street, some say it came from the old battery, other from behind a guard house & to the left of us.

Six of the penitent rebels again repenting left Col: McLean's corps: two of them knock'd down & disarm'd a Canadian sentry & the six escaped over the wall behind the artillery barracks. This morning the remaining eighty four were shut up. It appears that they all intend to run away. We took them in arms, they are rebels still in appearance, yet if there is one among them who wishes not to return to the Rebels it is hard on him to be confin'd

—but as we cannot read their hearts, prudence says keep them close.[36]

Some people have been seen in their old battery to day: a man in green (supposed to be a deserter from Town) was directing the view of four or five others, he pointed principally towards Cape Diamond. It is recommended in orders, that the officers & men not on guard to meet arm'd every evening at the Recollets, there to form a general Picquet. they are to sleep in their cloaths.

17TH   Westerly wind clear & cold weather. Some shot pierc'd Menuts house to day. The extra or voluntary general piquet to be at Mr Collin's & Mr Drummond's houses, as the most convenient & nearest the Ramparts.

Smoke seen in the chimney at Dr. Mabanes country house—there have not been any signs of people there since Decbr: last—some 32 lb shot wh we fir'd at it went over, the distance may be 2400 yds.

18TH   Wind Westerly exceeding cold. We fir'd a few shot at random into St John suburbs last night to keep off the Rebels—this evening a fire broke out there, & before day seven houses were burnt to the ground.

Our sentries were fir'd at: we saw nobody—we sent grape & Canister shot at random among the houses.

There is a white flag flying at Menuts to day—every day there is a number of Carioles at the door.

19TH   Moderate weather wind at S W, the suburbs of St Johns burning.

Every gun in the garrison was scal'd to day, there are one hundred & twelve fit for action besides Mortars Howitzers Royals & Cohorns.

20TH   Fine clear weather, the wind Westerly & cold. At ten at night the house nearest but one to St Johns gate was set on fire—nobody was seen altho the distance from our sentries is not fifty paces: many more houses were burnt—in short the whole is very near consum'd.

21ST   A Cloudy louring mild morning, wind at W. About seven o'clock a party of a hundred men commanded by Major Nairne took post in St Johns suburbs to prevent the Rebels from doing any further mischief.

In the forenoon twelve shot were fir'd from the enemies guard house west of the suburbs of St Johns—there is a rising ground which covers the suburbs from the West. Guns fir'd at that house must be much elevated to throw shot into Town. It is probable they have remov'd their guns from the Old battery—we saw two men there. The suburb is quite exposed to it, they wou'd have fired on Capt Nairnes party if they had had guns. We ply'd the Rebels to day with shot & shells.

In the afternoon we saw two men crossing the ice from the Canardiere towards Sault au Matelot; they halted half way as if afraid to proceed. An officer was sent to encourage them to come in, but our sentries by mistake fir'd at the officer & the two men ran back. In the evening 110 men under Colonel Caldwell re-liev'd Major Nairne.

22D   The northern lights made the night as bright as day almost. To day the wind is N E the weather cold. Fire wood brought in from St Johns suburb.

23D   There was no guard at St Johns last night. Westerly wind to day lowering & cold. About 4 this morning drums were heard at Menuts, St Foix &cc.

Rockets were seen in the night at the General Hospital & Beauport.

The Piquet made a sortie at St Johns gate before six in the morning to cover a wooding party. At sunset a number of men were seen near their guard house in St Roc. They got under cover as soon as they saw the fire of our guns.

A great many families supplied themselves with wood to day.

24TH   Wind S W fine moderate weather. In the night a deserter came to the walls, we drew him into Town by ropes he reports that "a man call'd Clinton stil'd General commands the Rebels; four hundred men from Montreal have join'd him—General Lee was order'd to march with 3000 men to Quebec—that order was soon countermanded, he march'd to Long Island to oppose Gov: Tryon who heads a body of 3000 Royalists well entrench'd— some ships had arriv'd at N: York with foreign Troops.[37]

"Gen: Schuyler was next destin'd for Canada, but the Congress sent him against Sr John Johnston, who was at the head of 500 friends of Government, at Johns Town on the Mohawk River.[38]

"Parties of 20, 30, 40 men have arriv'd from time to time at Montreal.

"The lakes are passable sooner this year than they have been for many years past.

"It is reported among the Rebel Privates, that there is an order of the Congress to break the first Officer who shall propose to storm Quebec, nevertheless 800 ladders were order'd to be made.

"A great many women & children (soldiers wives) perished in their way over the lakes in a late season.

"At Montreal the Militia Officers have been commanded to deliver up their Commissions which they receiv'd from Gen: Carleton, those who do not comply with this order are to be sent Prisoners to Hartford. He says that this is a manifest breach of faith in the rebels, & loudly complain'd of as such by many among themselves.

"None of the Gentlemen who were honour'd with the General's Commission, have been so mean as to give it up—the Rebels have 16 pieces of cannon none above 12 pounders.

"Duggan the barber in dudgeon has gone to lay before the Congress his great services, & to demand the reward of his merit."

25TH   Wind at N E warm & pleasant. The rebels from their guard house west of St Johns suburbs threw six 12 lbs shot into Town. A great quantity of firewood was got in to day.

We counted 49 men arm'd in Indian file walking on snow

shoes on the point Levy side; many sleighs follow'd them. The people all around us seem in motion.

26TH   Wind N E dark sleeting weather, not cold. We look'd for an attack last night, the weather being favourable. The Garrison was ready.

A person went out this evening for Orleans, he will return in a day or two.

The barking of dogs in every quarter without the walls was very remarkable, there is certainly some movement among the Rebels.

27TH   An air of wind at S E close damp warm weather.

Just before day many signals were made by fire in the adjacent Parishes.

Two men came so near the walls at Cape Diamond as to be heard distinctly call Good morrow Gentlemen. Drums were heard toward St Foix, & a regular platoon firing for a short while.

Voices which we imagin'd to be behind the Rebels battery were heard singing out as Sailors do when they hoist a great weight.

28   Wind S E with sleet and rain—a thorough thaw. A Canadian came in at Sault au Matelot—he say's he is but 13 days from Chambly. Colonel McLean says he is an honest man, who render'd him some very essential services last Fall.

He is come to give General Carleton all the information he cou'd gather; he has heard that "General Amherst is at N. York with 10,000 men from England."

"A person was sent by the Congress to take command of the Rebel army after Mr Montgomery's death—he arrived at Montreal, but return'd disgusted in two days. He declin'd having anything to do with men who had broken thro their solemn engagements with the Royalists at Montreal. He found that some of the Citizens had been imprisoned & some sent to Hartford."[39]

"About 200 sleighs were sent from Montreal early in January to bring the baggage of an expected reinforcement over the

Lakes. They all return'd empty at the months end—& only 160 men had arrived."

"The rebels have confess'd that the affair on the 31st of December lessen'd their number 750.

"Those who remain are afraid to go off since the Canadians have sworn that they will cut them to pieces in their retreat, if they do not make another effort to take the Town."

"It was industriously reported in every Parish in Canada immediately after the attack, that we had taken sixty Canadian prisoners, hang'd them over the ramparts without allowing them time to say, Lord have mercy on me—& we threw their bodies into the ditch exposed to the Dogs.

"The New England gentry shew very little knowledge of the Canadian Habitant, in imagining that this story wou'd rouse the Country people to arms, they cannot more effectually serve us than by propagating such falshoods."

"The Canadians keep up a very unremitted Patrole to cut off all communication with the Town."

"General Amherst has summon'd the members of the Congress to deliver themselves up."

"The Commander has issued out orders to the different Parishes near the town to provide Quarters for 7000 men."

29TH   High S W wind, cold weather.

Many arm'd men with knapsacks seen marching from Beauport towards the General Hospital in the Evening.

1ST   Wind cold at N W

In the afternoon some people were seen on the other side St Charles's river opposite to Mr Drummonds distillery. One shot from the 24 pounder behind the Hotel Dieu sent them off; about seven in the evening a house almost under that gun, & near the Still house was perceiv'd to be on fire, the flames quickly encreased & it burnt with great fury—it is probable that it was set on fire by the wadding which perhaps fell on the top of the house & the wind may have blown it up, for the roof was first in a blaze.

Some think that the Rebels may have set it on fire, in hopes that the flames wou'd catch the Distillery which wou'd certainly fire the Piquets above it, & from them the flames might be communicated to the Sailors Barracks in Montcalms house, & so the Conflagration might become general.

2D   Towards the morning 6 or 7 muskets were fir'd at our sentries in St Roc.

The person who was sent to Orleans on the 26th of last month has not yet got back: it is likely that the Canadian Patrole has got hold of him.

3D   West wind, fine clear cold weather. the voluntary picquet is reduced until the moon ceases to light us thro the night.

Three of the Emigrants deserted in the Evening—a party traced their footsteps in the snow; they fled towards the Rebels guard house in St Roc.

4TH   Thawing weather with a soft easterly wind. At three this morning, a rocket at P: Levy was answer'd by a cannon at St Foix.

We cut two deep trenches in the snow in the ditch at Cape Diamond.

In the evening we threw fire balls from a mortar; they gave great light.

A composition was hung over the angle at Cape Diamond; it burnt steadily & threw much light around: when it was almost consum'd there were sent from it hand grenades and bullets—fragments of metal flew about in all directions.

5TH   A strong wind at N E heavy sky drizly cold. This morning we discover'd a red flag flying on a pole stuck in a fence near Mr Lynd's farm, not far from the General Hospital—and another at the guard house at the west end of St Roc.

In new England the 5 of March is a day of fasting & prayer; aniversary orations are spoken in sad commemoration of what they call the bloody Boston Massacre.[40]

The greatest part of the Americans detest revenue officers. The board of Customs is deem'd an anticommercial institution.[41] The people of America stand up for an uncontroul'd trade—but the board was established to restrain an unlimited Traffic, & the Custom house officers often incensed the Boston mob by making siezures of countraband goods—they were often insulted in the streets, & they say that the lives of the most obnoxious (that is the Vigilant officers) were threaten'd.

There were frequent riots, tumults, & scuffles, & the Magistrates were unable to quell these disorders. They were forc'd to call in military aid to assist the Peace officer; at last some people were killed in the streets in an affray by the Kings troops, & perhaps the innocent unfortunately fell.

This transaction was painted in the most horrid colours, the account of it was published in the most moving language—the tragic tale was dispers'd in sheets blazon'd round with bones, deaths' heads & coffins, to rouse the indignation of the peaceful Farmer. Their pulpits rang with the cruelty of the minions of a blood thirsty Minister, who sent his Troops to enforce his arbitrary Laws meant to enslave the freeborn Sons of America.

On the return of this day, yearly sermons are preach'd to the People, that the seeds of a deadly enmity which these Messengers of God (as they call themselves) have sown, in a soil which they have been long preparing, may grow up to a plentiful harvest of Rebellion, against the Mother Country.

It has long been the policy of the Demagogues of N England to enflame the minds of the people against the Parent state to further their schemes of an Independency; that wild scheme will end in the ruin of all its abettors—the deluded multitude will see their error when alas! twill be too late. Their posterity will execrate the detested memory of those who are at this day, by an unaccountable infatuation regarded as the Fathers of their Country.

Allow the imaginary evils of the Americans to be real; have they a right to take up arms against their mother country to avenge themselves of the attempts of any faction who studies to oppress them? they blame not the nation at large. May we not address them in Veturia's speech to her Son Coriolanus who because he was unjustly banish'd Rome, join'd the Volsci & took arms against his country. Disclaiming against those at the helm of affairs he says to his mother

> Those walls contain the most corrupt of men,
> A base seditious herd: who trample order,
> Distinction, justice, laws, beneath their feet
> Insolent foes to worth, the foes of Virtue.

> *Veturia*

> Thou has not thence a right to lift thy hand,
> Against the whole community, which forms
> Thy ever sacred Country—that consists
> Not of Coeval Citizens alone:
> It knows no bounds; it has a retrospect
> To ages past; it looks on those to come;
> And grasps of all the general worth & Virtue.
> Suppose, My Son, that I to thee had been
> An harsh obdurate parent, even unjust:
> How wou'd the monstrous thought with horror strike thee
> Of plunging from revenge, thy raging steel
> Into her breast who nurs'd thy Infant years.[42]

The leaders of the American rebellion, & their abettors in England have by false informations, kept the lower class of people in ignorance. They firmly believe that the people in Britain are ready to take arms to force a repeal of the Acts which the Americans complain of.

In justice & in mercy, Great Britain will compel her Colonists to be happy, by enforceing submission to her Parliament.

Their eyes will soon be open'd, they'll return to their duty, & be convinc'd that their very existance as a free people, depends on the protection of the Mother Country.

It is propos'd to raise a company of Invalids in Town. Some people from real ailments, have been incapable of doing garrison duty, but there are many shameless beings within the walls, who under pretence of bad health, skulk from their duty & sleep soundly at home, while their fellow Citizens watch exposed to the rigours of a Canadian Winter.

Such as are found able to bear arms who have hitherto play'd the Valetudinarian from laziness, or from a motive more reprehensible, will be drawn out to publick view, they will be enrolled with the Invalids.

They can guard prisons, posts out of danger, since no manly feelings have stimulated them to do the duty of good subjects hitherto.

Hail rain at night.

One of the prisoners in the Recollets was put under close confinement for abusing a sentry and uttering some imprudent threats, "In a few days" said he among other things, "I shall be sentry over you, then I shall know how to use you."

6TH   It raind in the night—the wind is S W to day & it rains still— to walk in the streets is next to impossible: the ridges are cover'd with clear ice, & between them the water stands in Ponds knee deep.

7TH   Wind S W variable weather snowing & shining by turns. Fatigue parties are cutting trenches in the snow which lies deep in the ditch.

Men have been seen carrying boards over the heights from towards Wolfe's cove. A party of twenty men was sent on the look out, from the brow of the steep overlooking L'ance de Mer, they saw about 30 men at work there—on our first fire they all ran away.

Tis said we killed a man at a miles distance by one of our wall pieces to day.

The rebels appear in small groups of three four or five sauntring within four or five hundred yards of the wall, a discharge of grape shot convinces them where they are, they don't stay for a second.

On the highest part of Cape Diamond we erected a mast of 30 foot high, with a sentry box atop, from whence we can discover all that passes near Holland house their head quarters, & all the road as far as St Foix church lies open to our view.

The rebels hung out their red flag again to day near the Wind mill at St. Roc—some say tis a Squaws blanket border'd with black tape—others say, wringing their hands, *Mon Dieu c'est la Pavilion Sanglante.*

8TH   A mild morning, the wind at S W, the red black border'd flag is up to day. About four oclock this afternoon a foolish fellow named Robitaille came in from Lorrette—he knows nothing.

In the night two men Lamotte & Papinot Canadians, came over the ice from the Island of Orleans: it was with much difficulty that they cou'd keep out of the way of the Canadian Patrole: they keep constant rounds to guard every pass to Town —when they heard them near they threw themselves all along on the snow, & cover'd themselves with new white blankets; they came sometimes so near them that they cou'd hear what they said.

Mr Lamotte is but 11 days from Montreal & thirty from N: York—he has been in New England—the news he brings is not unfavourable for the King's loyal subjects, it gives us here a better prospect, than that we have had for sometime past.

It is said that he has brought letters from Governor Tryon to General Carleton.

"He reports that it was rumour'd as he came along that the rebels had attempted to storm Boston & that they had lost 4000 men in the attack, advancing on the ice it broke & let the greatest part of them in."

"The Colonists look forward & are dispirited, they raise recruits for the army at Cambridge with great difficulty, he saw many on their march to Head quarters weak sick & ill clad."

"The want of wollens is allready severely felt all over the continent: the thinking part now know that all the wool in America cou'd not furnish its inhabitants with stockings. The reinforcement for Canada assembled very slowly: first & last there may have arriv'd at Montreal between four or five hundred—but few or rather no more are expected.

"A hundred men better appointed than the rest were sent to garrison Quebec, but when they arrived at Montreal & found that General Carleton was in possession of the Capital, sixty of them return'd & forty of them laid down their arms saying—"*the service in which we engaged cannot be performed by us before Quebec is brought under the subjection of the Congress.*"

"There was lately a quarrel among the Rebels, they fought in the streets of Montreal.

"It is the common talk among them that they will storm the Town on the fifteenth of this month. Cash is very scarce among them, the Canadians are very averse to take their paper."

"Moses Hazen who was a Captain of Rangers at the taking of Quebec, a fam'd partizan remark'd by Gen: Wolfe for a good soldier, has dwindled down to a Colonel in the Rebel army—he has rais'd a hundred & fifty Canadian blackguards the first of his battalion—Edward Antil a Lawyer of Montreal is his Lieut: Colonel."[43]

"John Wells a merchant of Quebec acts for Price the rebel Comissary, who with Thos: Walker the noted Montreal Justice is gone to Philadelphia to give evidence before the Congress against Brigadier General Prescot, accus'd of having burnt Walkers house, & for confining him for traiterous conspiracies against the state."

"The Montreal Gentlemen who refus'd to give up their commissions in the Militia have been sent from thence & confin'd at Chambly, among whom are Monsieur Dufy, Monsieur St. George, & Mr. Gray."

He heard nothing of the troops which Chabotte (the man who came in some time ago) said were landed at N York.

Our sentries at Cape Diamond hear like people at work at a distance under the hill by the water side in the night.

We have for some time perceived small parties marching —countermarching between Beauport & the General Hospital.

The people in town who are really invalids join'd to those who pretend to be ailing were brought on the Parade to day; a hundred & eighty in number: above a hundred of them were found very fit for service in case of an attack—they were enroll'd

& the command of them given to Capt. Joseph Francois Cugnet.[44]

We saw flashes & heard the reports of muskets fir'd on the ice between the Town and Beauport, we suppose the Patrole has fir'd on some people attempting to get to Town.

9TH   Wind to the Norward of West, cold clear—there fell above two inches of snow last night: the river is not very full of floating ice, the outmost vessels in the Cul de Sac have their sterns free—some men have been seen in the old battery to day.

We have begun to build a barrier with cakes of ice to obstruct the enemies approach towards Lymburners battery in the Lower Town.

This day we have 114 pieces of cannon mounted in the Garrison— none under six pounders are counted: there is a great number of small guns, mortars, howitzers, Cohorns &cc.[45]

10TH   Wind Westerly clear & cold, The Picquets have orders to assemble at retreat beating.

The Garrison was alarm'd about ten oclock this evening— the drums beat to arms, the bell rang & a reinforcement was detach'd to Cape Diamond, from the Parade, where the Militia, British and Canadian, assembled in a very few minutes.

Two sentries without the ditch at Cape Diamond saw, as near as they cou'd guess, 200 men advancing up a hollow pass leading from L'ance de Mer—they halted on hearing a noise on the ramparts, stood a minute or two, wheel'd about & march'd back; In about half an hour the people were order'd home.

It was imagin'd that the prisoners wou'd be very troublesome in case of an alarm, but both officers & private men put out their lights & went to bed.

11TH   Wind at W cold & clear. The General review'd the British Militia on the Parade they had their arms in excellent order, & look'd very well considering all things.

A deep and wide trench was cut in the ice at Lymburners wharf.

A ditch was dug in the snow near the curtain at St Louis gate.

Fire balls were hung over all the angles, two were lighted; they answer'd well, they gave great light in the ditch, & shav'd the faces of the Bastions.

A sailor attempted to desert from his guard at Saut au Matelot in the night—the guards in St Roc near Palace gate took him up.

12TH   In the night the wind was N E there fell near a foot of snow—afternoon it was windy & cold— some of the Rebels have been sauntring about on the heights to day: Our sentries have been fir'd at.

13TH   A fine clear day, sharp air—wind N W. It is reported that "the Indians in the upper Countries have proposed among themselves to come down to the relief of this place." And that the peasants have "thrown out hints that they will not suffer the rebels to retreat."

These rumours may have sprung from certain intelligence, tho not to be credited.

Colonel M'Lean sent Capt: LittleJohn, master of a vessel, (now commander of a Province arm'd ship) with 17 seamen to look into L'ance de Mer.

The party came unexpectedly on a sentry, he fir'd his musket & roll'd himself down a steep hill among about 100 men at work on a beach; we fir'd on them, & they decamp'd in great confusion leaving their Jackets tools &cc behind them.

A few of them fir'd in their retreat, we were far above them —three of them fell, but whether thro fear, or from wounds we cannot say.

There is still a talk about fitting out two batteaus with six pounders in their bows, to row up and down, to observe the enemies motions near ye River.

When the wind blows from the West, the river on this side is quite free from ice, a birch canoe may sail without risk.

The prisoners who were incorporated with the Emigrants, but afterwards secur'd in the Recollets, were remov'd to a stronger place in the Artillery—those who did not enlist are lodg'd in the Dauphin barracks.[46]

14TH   Wind Easterly with a heavy sky: there fell a great deal of snow in the afternoon.

About 5 o clock in the evening a man in blue with buff facings, carrying what the Rebels call a flag of truce, with a drummer in front was seen coming from the guard house at the end of St Roc: he was permitted to advance as far as the angle at the two gun battery—he desir'd admittance, having letters for the Governor.

The General sent his Major of Brigade to inform him that he cou'd not be admitted, nor shou'd he be listen'd to but in imploring the Kings mercy—then said he I am ready to obey your commands—the Major said you are to return from whence you came: he wheel'd about, & walk'd away.

15TH   A very fine mild day, thawing much. A Canoe was sent with Capt: La force (a Canadian a Province arm'd schooner) on the look out: he kept well over on the Shore.[47] Two Canadians haild him—they ask'd if they might go to Town & be in safety; he assur'd them of a good & friendly reception; they said they wou'd go over next day.

Two men arriv'd in a canoe from Beauport in the night, they say "the Habitants below Point Levy are ready to take arms to drive the Bostonois out of the Country, they have no cash, they begin to hang their heads—they have long beat up for recruits, they have got about a hundred of the most idle profligate wretches in the Country—they have erected a battery at Point Levy opposite to Cul de Sac—they have a howitzer & one gun mounted."

Provisions for 1000 men have been lodged on the route; they look daily for that number from Montreal.

16TH   Wind N E a great deal of snow fell the last night—it rains excessively to day.

17TH   It rain'd all the night, wind S W to day still raining. The men from Beaumont say the rebels tell the country people that the plague is in town, & that in a short time there will be nobody left to bury the dead.

The voluntary piquets are at present very strong, every man not on guard sleeps in his cloaths with his musket by his side.

There's not a man in the Garrison who does not ardently wish that the Rebels may soon make an attempt to scale the walls —we know that we shall drive them off with great loss to them, & safety to ourselves.

No day in which men can stand out in the open air, passes without working parties, to clear the ramparts, & for other necessary fatigue.

Some of the Canadian Royalists of Point Levy (small is their number) told the Rebels in answer to some questions concerning the look out, we erected at Cape Diamond. "It is, said they, a wooden horse with a bundle of hay before him."

Gen Carleton has said that he will not give up the Town till the horse has ate the hay, & the General is a man of his word.

Six sentries one after another refus'd to stand sentry on Mr Drummonds wharf outside of Pres de Ville, some were afraid of riflemen, & others declar'd their dread of the ghosts of the men lately slain there, they were sent prisoners to the main guard. The Beaumont men return'd in the night carrying some late printed Gazettes—they will endeavour to pay us another visit soon.

From the look out in the afternoon we saw about 500 men drawn up at Holland house, & about 200 at Menuts.

18TH   Thawing weather wind at S W. The Canadian soldiers who refus'd to do their duty in Mr. Drummonds wharf, were this morning reprimanded on the Parade at guard mounting.

Two batteaus with guns are ready for launching—the wind is East this evening & our side of the River is full of ice.

From the look out we have seen crowds about Holland House, and on St Foix road.

19TH   Wind all the day N E, at night it clear'd up at W. Two batteaus & two cutters row'd up the River as far as Sillerie to reconnoitre. Major Nairne & Capt: Owen went out at the Sally Port at Cape Diamond with a party, & march'd to the hcight overlooking l'ance de Mer—they saw nothing.[48]

A batteau cross'd the river from Sillerie, something was hoisted out by a gin, probably it was a gun for the battery at Point Levy. Some men were seen near the old battery on the heights.

The rebel's sentries from St. Charles's (the little) River across Abrahams heights to the River St Lawrence to prevent deserters bringing us intelligence, they are posted within 200 yds of each other.

20TH   Cloudy weather, the air is Easterly.

About 4 o clock this morning a number of men were discover'd by the outside sentry, near the W end of St Johns suburbs, the Picquet was order'd out, on hearing the noise the rebels went off.

We saw twelve horses drawing something seemingly of great weight on the Point Levy side towards the place where the new battery is said to be, it is a mile from us.

We heard the report of a cannon somewhere near head quarters.

Canoes crossing over to Sillerie, they say there is a market kept there, the weather is very variable.

21ST   The wind is at N W, it froze very hard in the night, the cold continues.

Seven canoes nine men in each seen crossing over to Sillerie.

22D   Wind Easterly cold & cloudy; we plainly see people at work on the Point Levy side opposite to the Cul de Sac, they are driving stakes, & throwing up snow or earth; the distance may be between 1600 & 1700 yards.

We are busy laying platforms for some 32 pounders on the grand battery, & we are clearing away the snow from some 13 inch mortars.

We fir'd some shot & threw shells at those we saw at work. By the situation of this new battery we think that their principal aim will be at the shipping in Cul de Sac; they may perhaps intend to batter Pres de Ville & Saut au Matelot, if they have heavy metal, this we doubt. Our fire at all events must be infinitely superior to theirs.[49]

23D   It was very dark last night, but we kept a good look out —the wind is still easterly; no wood in the barrack yard—it snows.

24TH   The last night was darker than the former—the wind is at N W with a gloomy hard sky—the weather is intolerably cold.

25TH   N W wind, extremely cold.
    Chabotte the first man who came in with intelligence, gave us room to expect an attack before this day—we have been looking for the Rebels, & they will find us always ready to give them a proper reception.
    We made fire signals from the look out, & play'd off some rockets before day light at the two gun battery.
    The signals were understood from guard to guard.

26TH   The cold was inexpressibly intense last night—about two o clock this morning the Rebels made signals by fire at their guard house W of St Johns suburbs & fir'd a musket. We fir'd at their works at Point Levy, & threw some well directed shells. We perceive an extensive fascade of fascines. Two men walking on the ice from Orleans towards the Town were overtaken by a party from Beauport, & conducted that way. We are preparing to lay platforms near the Citadel, the guns to be mounted there will enfilade their battery.
    We saw a body of men of St. Foix road—we heard three chears.

27TH   Wind S W mild weather. This morning before day signal Rockets from Cape Diamond were answer'd by rockets at the Artillery barracks.
    The large house at the Canardiere where the rebels kept a guard, was burnt to the ground this morning: we saw people in great confusion endeavouring to save what was in the house.

Many arm'd men marching to & fro on the Point Levy side. Canoes & boats frequently crossing the river above the Town, but out of the reach of our guns.

Ninety six men in Indian file marching from the ferry at little river towards Beauport.

An arm'd batteau was sent up the river at ten at night— there was nothing seen.

28   All was quiet last night. Wind SW cold and hazy. Wind N W afternoon very cold.

29TH   Wind N W cold & clear last night. Bodies of men seen moving from different quarters towards the General Hospital— the Rebels battery at P Levy appears longer, we fir'd on the people at work there from the Chateau battery; we threw shells from the grand battery.

30TH   N Wind, a cold clear morning. A gin was seen in the P Levy battery, we threw those that were at work there into great confusion by our shot & shells.

We fir'd a gun at a groupe of seven men west of St Johns suburbs—one of them fell. Five men appear'd between Port Louis & Cape Diamond—some grape shot made them scamper, one of them was in blue fac'd with white. There was a large quantity of firewood got in at St Johns gate to day: people conceal'd behind the old battery fir'd on the wooding party—a few 36 lb shot made them silent.

Several detachments of thirties & forties were seen marching up from Montmorency.

Our sentry on the two gun battery overlooking St Roc saw a man endeavouring to conceal himself behind a wall there, a file of men went out & brought him in very drunk—he said he came from Pointe aux Trembles this morning, & that he had lost his way. He belongs to one of the 5 companies of Philadelphians which arriv'd to day—the rest are soon expected with the 2d Battalion: he seems to be an ignorant fellow, all that he says is, they are soon to scale the walls, & that there are but very few Canadians with them—Colonel Hazen getts no recruits. In the night a number of men advanc'd as far as the burying ground into St Johns suburbs.

31ST   Wind S W with snow—about two in the morning the sentries on Cape Diamond saw flashes of fire & heard reports of muskets—to them they appear'd as fir'd at Pres de Ville, the guards were alarm'd & the Picquets order'd out—on enquiry it was found that the firing was on the other side of the river.

The Prisoner we took yesterday is sober to day he adds nothing more than what he has already said.

The Jailor of the Dauphin barracks where the Rebel soldiers are confin'd, perceiv'd that a door in a vault which leads into the street had been forc'd. The lock & 2 hinges had been wrench'd off—the door hung by a third hinge wch had not been seen. Immediately enquiry was made into this matter.

The only Englishman among the whole Prisoners discover'd the whole: he said that some of them had conceal'd an old hatchet, & grop'd their way in the night into the vault; they inform'd the rest that they had done the work: that one pull at the door wou'd open a free passage into the street.

In that belief they laid their heads together to concert a plan to join their friends without the walls, in case they shou'd not be able to let them into Town—they began by chusing Officers to command in action—their plan was laid, first to surprise the 24 men on guard over them, sieze their arms and ammunition & proceed about 150 yards to St Johns gate, & disarm that guard also.

By some unaccountable means, they had found a way to send one of their number over the walls to inform Arnold of this plot, & to let him know that they wou'd put it in execution the first dark stormy night, praying him in all bad weather to be near St Johns gate with a strong force; he wou'd know that they were out of Prison, when the houses nearest that gate shou'd be in flames—they were to turn the cannon at St Johns gate against the Town, & immediately open a way for Arnold & his party.

If they shou'd find it impraticable to force the gate, they were to escape over the wall by ladders which they were to take from the roof of the barracks, & from the adjacent houses, & that the guns might not annoy them they were to throw spunges, rammer, wadding &cc into the ditch.

The Officers prisoners in the Seminary knew nothing of this affair.

The greatest part of those concern'd in this plot were put in irons; many of them behav'd very insolently on this occasion. Two of them pretend ignorance of the matter.

The General has order'd a feint to be made tomorrow morning at two o clock, in order to draw the rebels to an attack.

Some deserter may inform them that the Plot is discover'd, if a feint is not imediately made: every thing is to be carried on, as if the prisoners had made good their escape out of prison, & had got possession of St Johns Gate.[50]

At four o clock P M a deserter came in, he is of the first Battalion of Philadelphians, he says their company consists of 63 men—they desert dayly.

1ST   Wind at S W thawing much—hot sunshine.

At two oclock this morning every person not on guard was under arms on his alarm post. The walls were well lin'd—it was perfectly calm, unluckily the moon shone exceedingly bright—however bon fires were lighted near the walls a hot fire from musketry was kept up for ten minutes—a confus'd mixture of cries—three long loud huzzas were follow'd by a firing from two brass six pounders well serv'd, their muzzles turn'd towards the Town—the musketry still fir'd, & now & then 3 chears were given, this was continued for a considerable time—but no men appear'd without the walls. We saw no signals, nor did we hear any drums.

At day break every one was order'd home.

Altho the feint did not succeed (indeed the General was dubious of it's success) it will have a happy effect, it will shew the Rebels that we wish to see them—it will give them a dread to approch.

We can plainly see 4 embrasures in their battery at P Levy —perhaps some are mask'd by a long bank of snow to the right.

The deserter who came in yesterday says that in coming over the Lake he met many small parties, three four at a time leaving Canada; that a Lieutenant had deserted—they brought him back—he got away at last—he can clasp round the greatest gun they have. "Sometime ago two of our shells fell without bursting, those who pick'd them up sold the powder which they containd at a dollar per pound to the commanding officer, they have at this time but thirteen rounds."

In the afternoon another deserter came in—he says "they have but 15 men on guard at the W end of St Roc."

"This Morning's feint greatly alarm'd the Rebels, they stood under arms till 7 o clock."

The voluntary Piquet ceases to be general for a time. A Captain, 2 Subalterns, a Sergeant, a corporal, & 30 men were deem'd sufficient, in dark moon it will become general again.

2ND   Wind S W warm clear weather. Three men were seen near the ruins at Mount Pleasant about 400 yards from Port Louis; one of them wore a large grey periwig, suppos'd to be

David Wooster, another was dress'd in scarlet said to be Arnold, the third, said those who had good glasses was Edward Antil—they stood pointing to the walls probably planning an attack, which they never intend to make.[51]

A number of men 60 or 70 were seen exercising near the General Hospital—a single shot from the Town dispers'd them. Some men were seen as if at work near the old battery—several small parties have been seen marching to the different guard houses—some people aver that they can see ladders strew'd on the ground behind the old battery, & from the look out they are seen with their glasses much farther.

In the Evening a cutter was sent to look into Wolfes cove, she got inclosed by the ice, & was carried up by the tide—near the cove she was fir'd on from six pounders, & an arm'd bateau attempted to pursue her; our men broke their way thro the ice with the butt ends of their muskets & got away.

3D   Wind Easterly soft & cloudy. The Rebels open'd their battery of 5 guns at P. Levy about 8 o'clock this morning, they fire 24-12- & 9 lb shot—some of them did not reach to this side of the river—a 12 lb shot quite spent reach'd Palace street: their aim is at the shipping. they have hit the Lizzard Frigate— a ball has damag'd her foremast.

About midday we plainly heard the report of 5 guns at 2 or 3 leagues distance down the river: they seem to be large, but the present state of the atmosphere may deceive us in that particular.

One nam'd Chabott who had the command of a small arm'd schooner last fall, left vessel, guns & all on the Island of Orleans, where the ice had put her on shore; it is probable that she is now afloat, & in the hands of the rebels, perhaps they were her 3 pounders we heard. It is by four weeks too early to expect any thing up the river.

The Rebels threw 3 eight inch shells from P Levy—they did no damage.

We made many excellent shots to day; in short their fire soon slacken'd after our heavy flankers at the Citadel began to play.

Excessive heavy rain in the afternoon.

4TH   It rain'd all the night—the wind is S W—we keep up a hot fire upon the enemy—they give us a shot now & then—they have done us no harm as yet—we see but few people.

Ten rockets at the ferry house a mile on the other side of the little river were answer'd by the discharge of a gun at P Levy.

5TH   Wind this morning to the norward of West—very cold —an 8 inch shell burst above the shipping in Cul de Sac—a falling piece of it fractur'd a Sailors skull, they watch an opportunity, & fire a gun now & then, draw them behind the merlons, & get under cover.[52]

We threw some shells into their works, & made many good shots to day. A general fatigue clearing snow from the ramparts.

An hundred & one men march'd from Beauport to the ferry house; we sent some shot thro it.

Carried the timber of a block house without the walls to be erected between Port Louis & Cape Diamond.

Monsieur Loiseaux an honest Canadian came in at Saut au Matelot at ten this evening.

6TH   Easterly wind & heavy sky—a deserter came in this morning.

Mr. Loiseaux reports "that Gen: Lee was once actually on his way to Canada with 4000 men—he was seiz'd with the gout —a great many of his men deserted."

"Sixty Canadians at South River had taken arms, intending to surprise the guard at P Levy: their intention was discover'd to the rebels by some villain among themselves—their design was to join the Kings loyal subjects in Town.

"They were attack'd unawares when they were assembled at a Priests house—they fir'd on them. 5 of the Canadians fell— their fire killed 6 of the Rebels.

"Monsieur Bailly a very brave & loyal priest was dangerously wounded—he had two balls thro his body; 34 Canadians were sent prisoners to the Head quarters of the Rebels the rest made their escape.

"The Rebel General has order'd that all the Priests on

Orleans who dare to refuse absolution shall be sent Prisoners to Head Quarters.

"They have appointed one Lotbiniere a Priest, who is to give absolution to all who ask it—they allow him 1500 livres perannum: & they are to make him a Bishop when they take Quebec."[53]

They have amus'd the deluded Peasants with grants of houses in the City: these poor Devils will stake a house at a game at Brelan.

"The Habitants believe that it will be impossible for us to hold out many days longer, since the Rebels have told them, that they are to batter the Town from the heights & P Levy & to bombard us from the ferry house, but there are some among them who tremble lest they may not succeed.

"The rebels are sickly, many are under inoculation.

"There's a number of N: Yorkers in the Rebel army—their engagements with the Congress end on the 15th of this month; they have given great uneasiness at Holland house by their declarations: they say that on the 16th they'l lay down their arms & return homewards."

"The Rebels stopp'd two Gentlemen from N York on suspicion— they wou'd not allow them to proceed to Quebec: they had letters for Gen: Carleton, but no papers were found with them."

"We have disabled two guns on their battery, kill'd 3 men & wounded 2.

"They now fire two guns at a time, & these but seldom; & tho they fire red-hot balls they do us not the least damage."

"Our feint of the 1st made the Rebels very much out of humour, they say they were made April fools."

7TH   Rain Hail sleet with a N E wind. The Rebels fir'd a good many shots & some shells but did no hurt.

8TH   Southerly wind & soft weather. It has been a custom observ'd by the rebels for some days past to fire 4 guns & a howitzer, & leave their battery early, in the course of the day they steal down to give us a shot now & then. They can't stand our fire.

In the Evening a ricochet shot enter'd the window of a house in the upper Town, where the family sat round the tea table—the eldest boy of ten years, was struck on the head, & expir'd ere his mother cou'd catch him in her arms.

The roofs of some Churches & houses in the upper Town have received a little damage.

9TH   Easterly wind with drizling weather—much firing on our side very little on theirs. A decent looking man calling himself Chaucer came in to day—he talks a great deal, we gather from him that he is or was a butler—he says that Gen: Lee was on his march hither—but was order'd to N York to take the command there—the Rebels are about 1800 near Quebec of whom between six and eight hundred are in hospitals.

"They talk of storming the Town at Pres de Ville, Sault au Matelot & at Cape Diamond before the 15th. on which day the engagements of many of the men will finish."

"The N Yorkers are very highly incens'd at the behaviour & conduct of those they call the Yankeys—they mean the people of the 4 N England provinces, who they say affect a disgusting superiority, taking the lead in every thing."

"They are soon to open a battery against Port Louis at 500 yds distance, of 5 guns—9 & 12 pounders & they are to bombard us with 5 howitzers from the ferry house."

"They have two Gondolas afloat—they are busy preparing a fire vessel to burn the shipping in Cul de Sac."

"The Canadians are dissatisfied with the Rebel payments, they by no means take the Congress Paper, they are glad to exchange a handful of it for a dollar."

"They have punish'd a Canadian in an Arbitrary manner for speaking in favour of the Royalists.

"They have put Mr. Evans in irons for caning 2 or 3 insolent Montrealists who were holding forth in favour of the invasion of Canada. He was formerly an officer in the 28th Regt: he threaten'd to chastise some of the Rebel officers, they complain'd to their leader, & Mr Evans was sent prisoner to Hartford far from his family—their moderation & love of justice is very conspicuous.[54]

"Arnold is to leave the Camp tomorrow to hasten down the long look'd for reinforcement. The rebels have no shoes; In the present state of the roads he cannot reach Montreal in less than 3 or 4 days & a body of men will require 8 or 10 days to march down from thence unless they can be sent in Batteaus, at any rate they cannot be here before the 15th—on which day or rather before they threaten to storm us—we are ready to receive them.

We now guard on the river every night. Our wharfs are garnish'd with guns—we have cannon in some vessels in the Cul de Sac, & strong guards in the Lower Town.

Our voluntary Picquets continue, no man sleeps at home— we assemble every night together ready to repulse wherever attacks may be made.

Mr. Chaucer is suspected, he will be properly taken care of.

10TH   Wind Westerly soft weather,—the streets are full of water, the snow under it is porous & rotten—if one steps out of the beaten path, he sinks to the knee.

If the rebels shou'd attempt to approach the walls in the present state of the snow, especially when loaden with ladders, they will be mowed down by our grape & canister shot.

A young man nam'd Pepper came down from Cap Rouge this morning—he confirms what Chaucer has said concerning the discontentment of the N: Yorkers, & the uneasiness of the Canadians.

The Rebels now despairing of success have thrown off the mask. Instead of Candour & Moderation which they say is the Characteristic of the Sons of Liberty—as they call themselves— disingenuity & oppression mark them.

This young mans Father is among the Rebels, they have press'd him to accept of the Command of a Gondola.

They propose destroying the Vessels in the Cul de Sac, by running the fire ship full sail among them.

11TH   A strong wind at N E with heavy rain. The battery at

P Levy is silent to day: those who know the ground say that it is situated in a swampy hollow.

We made some fine shots.

At midnight the guards at Cape Diamond St Johns & Palace Gate made their signals to each other by rockets—about ten o'clock last night 3 were play'd off at Holland house, Menuts, & the ferry house.

12TH   Thawing, Easterly, sleeting weather.
Fire balls were lighted at the Angles to illuminate the ditch, & the faces of the Bastions. They burnt all night. Many shot were fir'd at our shipping to day—very little damage was done.

13TH   Wind W cold lowring weather. Fire balls were lighted at one & continued unto 3 this morning—Signal Rockets from guard to Guard.

A shot from P Levy went thro the Cabin window of the Hunter sloop of war.

The prisoners who were secur'd in irons after their plot to escape was discover'd, have found means to procure files, they have fil'd off the rivets of their handcuffs, & put on leaden ones in their stead.

A court of enquiry sat on the Master of a vessel—he had charge of the guns near Palace gate; the Officer who reliev'd him from that guard found a nine pounder filled with rubbish. He was acquitted.

Where we perceive men at work to day, about 800 yds from Port Louis, a battery will be cover'd from any guns on our walls —but the 32 pounders on the Cavaliers will tear their works to pieces.[55] We fir'd some shot from Port Louis which did not disturb them.

14TH   It froze hard last night—the weather is warm to day with a clear W wind. Fire balls were lighted, & rocket signals made as usual. The shot from P Levy are all aim'd at Cul de Sac to day, a ball went into the Lizzards stern, another hurt the main mast of a large transport.[56]

Chaucer has repeatedly said, we shall be attack'd by the

15th—this then must be the night. We shall have 1500 men ready to receive them.

A Blockhouse about 100 yds from Port Louis outside was finish'd to day—it will be strongly guarded to night—the people all around are in motion this evening.

15TH   Last night was clear & frosty: everything remain'd quiet: this morning the wind is Westerly with cloudy weather. the number of people that we saw in motion round us yesterday, some at Holland house, & a party advancing towards St Roc made us imagine that an attack was intended as Chaucer had said.

Before day light as usual fire balls were lighted, and the guards pass'd their signal Rockets. In the afternoon the Sailors song was heard on the plains, they were moving in a heavy body, in the evening a great concourse of people were seen at Menuts: they gave 3 chears. It is suppos'd by many that the N Yorkers have renewed their engagements; others think that they have declar'd off, & to encourage those who remain the officers may have been haranguing them, to shew them what glory & how much booty every man wou'd have, on entering in triumph the Town of Quebec, which the private men are taught to believe must fall, we shall suppose that, elevated with hope, they gave three chears.

At nine at night guns were fir'd & signals made from the Point of Orleans; we imagine that the guard there was alarm'd by a drifting Shallop which pass'd the Town about dusk.

16TH   Last night was mild & so clear that the fire balls were not necessary. Rocket signals as usual.

We had strong guards in the block houses outside of Cape Diamond & Port Louis. The wind is strong at E to day—the Rebels did not fire a gun—we fir'd at both their batteries, we have measur'd the distance of the last erected & find it to be 716 yds 2 feet.

17TH   Wind N E. There fell 2 inches of snow in the night— at one in the morning fireballs were lighted, signals made by rockets. The Rebels at work on the heights. Canoes & bateaus passing & repassing opposite to Sillery full of men—the enemy fir'd none to day.

Afternoon Capt Laforce went up the river in a canoe to reconnoitre: he kept the other shore aboard—he was hailed by some Canadians—he asked them why they did not come to Town —they answer'd they had no canoes, & that they were closely watch'd, they press'd him to come ashore, but aware of P Levy treachery he bid them bon soir.

18TH   Wind S W showers of snow. Fire balls & rockets at the usual hour. The Rebels fir'd from P Levy very early. Canoes crossing to the P. Levy side, full of men.

The snow has melted so much that we find a second crop of Picquets in St Roc; a large quantity of firewood was got in to day.

Two deserters came in this afternoon who report that "the N Yorkers to the number of 300 had been assembled on the 15th —every argument had been us'd to persuade them to renew their engagements, but these men predetermin'd every solicitation, were immoveable.

"To all the entreaties used, they answer'd, that the Congress had deceiv'd them—they as yet had no pay— they had in a manner been forc'd to renew their first engagements, but they had resolv'd not to enter into a third, they see their error, & are firmly determin'd never to fire a shot against the Kings friends —their spokesmen ended with a *God Save the King* which was echoed by one & all of them with three chears.

"Immediately their drums beat to arms orders were given to secure the Mutineers—they were seiz'd, very ill used & confin'd; the rebellious Canadians were the most forward in this service."[57]

The Rebels not including the Canadians are 1800—600 of them or more are sick, & scatter'd up & down—

"They still assure the Canadians that a reinforcement is at hand, & they promise that all those who shall assist in storming the Town shall have their share of the plunder.

"Nothing will tempt the Habitants forward but a prospect of the great booty.

"There is not a single man within the walls that does not most heartily wish that the Rebels may attack us."

We know what kind of a reception they will meet with—they know it also, it keeps them back, notwithstanding their gasconades [boastings].

Their leaders are perpetually telling them that they will march them to an easy conquest—but why do they not advance?

They have not forgotten the 31st of Decemr: the Canadians will ever remember it.

"It is whisper'd in their camp that 2 ships have been seen in the river, to their great dismay."

The ice from Lake St Peter above Three Rivers pass'd the Town to day.

19TH   Every thing remain'd very quiet last night—it froze very hard—fire balls & rockets a l'ordinaire—the day is cloudy & cold with the wind at S W.

A few shots from P Levy were aim'd at the ships in Cul de Sac.

20TH   Two men who left Quebec last fall came down from Cape Rouge in a canoe, they say that the Rebels have turned the Gaspey arm'd Brigantine into a fire ship, & have offer'd 20,000 livres to any person who will steer her into Cul de Sac, & then set fire to the train.

No Yankey, no N Yorker, nor ere a Canadian has as yet offer'd his service; An Accadian has said that he will perform it for 30,000 lb *en bon argent sonnant* [in good ringing silver].

Colonel Caldwell with the 8th Regiment is on his march from Niagara with a number of Indians: it was not to hurry down the reinforcement that Arnold posted away to Montreal but to oppose Col: Caldwell.[58]

We have almost finish'd the 5 gun battery behind the Hotel Dieu, the 24 lbers planted there will bear on their works at the ferry house—we have already done it considerable damage, we have often seen it full of arm'd men.

It is whisper'd that some of the Town's people who abandon'd in consequence of the Generals Proclamation, have been very busy in improving the Rebellious disposition that shews itself in the Country—they have told the Habitants that unless they will heartily assist the Bostonois—Slavery, abject slavery will be their portion.

Chaucer is a spy say these men—he was made an officer just before he came into Town, he promis'd to return in 3 days if alive.

One of the Prisoners in the seminary found means to send letters to the Head Quarters of the Rebels, agreeing on signals, by which their friends within the walls shou'd know whenever any reinforcement shou'd arrive, & the number of men; as also the time of an attack if any shou'd be intended, that they might if possible cooperate with them.

21TH   A clear serene night preceded a fine day, wind at S W.

The Rebels beat to arms at 3 in the morning.

The battery on the heights does not (that we can see) advance.

At the hour of going to mass they fir'd on the Town—a diabolical spirit! mean they to kill women & helpless children. They see plainly that they can make no kind of impression upon the Town.

Hitherto they have kill'd a boy—wounded a Sailor, & broke the leg of a Turkey.

Swallows were seen to day. The fire we keep upon the ferry house allows no rest to the Rebels lodg'd thereabout; the guns behind the Hotel Dieu—the two gun battery & the guns higher up near St Johns gate all bear on the ferry house.

At dusk Capt La force's arm'd schooner mann'd with 30 fine fellows, was haul'd out into the stream, the Rebels fir'd at her from P Levy & beat to arms—she was let drive up to Pres de Ville with the tide & then dropt anchor, a body of floating ice broke her cable, & she was carried up as far as Wolfe's cove—the Lizzard sent a boat after her with a cable & Anchor, which arriv'd in good time for she was very near the shore—the Rebel guards fir'd on them—the schooner directed by their fire gave them grape & Canister in return

22D   The last night was soft & serene. Fire balls were lighted at one, & they burnt until day. Wind N E with snow.

The Rebels open'd their battery at the ferry this morning between 9 & 10 o clock with 2 guns—they have cut embrasures thro a very thick breast work which the French army threw up in 1759, they fir'd between 30 & 40 shot. We have mounted two French 26 pounders, behind the Hotel Dieu, we have in all 5 there, which batter their works & the ferry house a few paces behind them.

The enemy keeps close, their shot have hurt the chimneys & roofs of some houses—they are far below us, & are oblig'd to elevate their guns. The red black bound flag which has hung out since the 5th of March was taken down last night, some say that by striking this flag they wou'd intimate to their friends, that no more reinforcement is expected.

23RD   There has fallen above 3 inches of soft sloppy snow since yesterday morning—it was dark and lowring all the night—& favourable for an attack. The Garrison was not unwatchful.

A canoe was brought to by Capt La forces schooner—she was from Montreal. Signal rockets were sent from all the guards facing the plains. Fire balls as usual.

There was six men in the canoe from Montreal, one of the number Monsieur Rousseau left N York 27th March. A report prevail'd at that time that 27 sail of ships had been seen off Rhode Island, & that the Kings troops had evacuated Boston to go to N York, & that Lord Stirling was to oppose their landing with a great force.[59]

A reinforcement has been sent from Boston to this place.

"He pass'd Mr Thomas (formerly an apothecary now a General) at the head of 1200 as a reinforcement for the Rebel army in Canada. On the 3d of this month their advanc'd guard were at Still Water 27 miles on this side of Albany; he found 80 bateaus waiting for them at Ticonderoga—Lake George was not passable when he was there."

"They bring six iron twenty four pounders along with them, which detain them very much.

"It has been reported in Albany in terror, & confidently

talk'd of at Montreal that Colonel Caldwell with the 8th regiment, & a number of Indians are on their way down from the upper Country.

"If a number of bateaus cou'd have been procur'd above 600 Canadians wou'd have come down to the relief of Quebec, when this canoe came away." Gen: Lee is gone to Virginia.

The Rebels fir'd a great deal from P Levy & from the ferry battery—we made a great number of good shots at both: a few chimney's have been damag'd to day.

About ten oclock at night the rebels threw 6 small shells from the last erected work on the heights: they were aim'd at the block houses outside of the walls, but they all fell short—we sent 6 13 & 10 inchers in return.

Signal Rockets as usual.

24TH   Last night was clear and cold; the wind shifted to N W where it continues with delightful weather.

The Rebels fir'd red hot balls to day—their fire is much slacken'd—ours much encreas'd—their works must be very much destroy'd—they are reduc'd to one gun at the ferry—we saw them carry off some men wounded or killed. They continue to fire on our shipping from P Levy.

25TH   It did not freeze last night: signal rockets in the morning as usual.

The little river is now clear of ice the rebels must now cross over above the ferry, or be expos'd to the shot. They remember that they had a Sergeant killed by a 12 lb shot in crossing in the flat in Novemr: last.

We mounted a 24 pounder to day to bear on their battery opposite to Port Louis, from their works they can only see roofs & chimneys.

The wind shifted to N E it blew & rain'd excessively hard: there was very little firing on either side.

We heard the reports of great guns from below, twelve or fourteen; some people flatter themselves with hopes that they were fir'd on board a ship of war—others think they may have been from Chabotts schooner or from a Brigantine of Arnolds which had winter'd below.

26TH   The last night the weather was intolerably bad, the wind was violent at N E with a deluge of rain—it continued all day. This evening the rebels fire from both their batteries. We give them 3 guns for one.

Capt La force chas'd some canoes; they got ashore & the people ran into the bushes—he call'd after them upbraiding them for not coming into Town—some of them ventur'd to the waters edge, & answer'd that they had a strong inclination to go to Quebec, but that they dar'd not stir from home, because their houses will be set on fire if they be absent but for a day, & all their effects will be seized—this is another sample of American moderation! their system of liberty is admirable! their regard for justice is very glaring!

The Habitants have no right to complain if the rebels shou'd opress them—why did they suffer them to set foot in the Province.

Mr La force told them that now or never was the time for them to retrieve their character, a few days wou'd stigmatize them for Rebels & Cowards—they made no answer.

27TH   It was very foggy all last night—we cou'd not see across the ditch from the embrasures, we were therefore much on our guard—this is a clear morning.

At one oclock just after the different guards had answer'd each others signals by rockets, 5 guns were fir'd from the ferry battery. We began to cast longing eyes towards P Levy, we hope soon to see ships from England.

A prisoner, one of the Rebel Capts: was sent from the Seminary to the main guard for attempting to make his escape.

The sentry at the further angle of Cape Diamond about ten oclock at night call'd out *a fire ship, a fire ship,*—this gave the alarm—the great bell of the Cathedral, & all the other bells in Town were set a ringing—the drums beat to arms; the garrison was posted in a few minutes; the fire ship prov'd to be a house or a heap of rubbish in a blaze on the beach on the P Levy side. On this discovery every man was order'd back from whence he came.

The rebels fir'd a great deal to day, we sent them 10 balls for one, & some shells.[60]

28TH It froze a little last night—fine weather this morning, wind at W; there has been but little firing on either side to day.

29TH Serene mild weather, wind at S W—four muskets fir'd on the heights before day.

Red hot balls fir'd into town.

30TH A small breeze at E with soft rain in the morning—fog with heavy rain in the afternoon.

Two soldiers flush of money were question'd of their serg-eants; after many contradictory tales they were threaten'd with confinement if they wou'd not immediately reveal how they had got so many dollars.

They at last confess'd that they had been brib'd by some of the Rebel Officers to assist them in making their escape—the plan was laid & to be put in execution the first time they were on guard at the Seminary, if unhappily any one shou'd be found in their way they were to have been dispatched without mercy.

They were to have let themselves drop over the wall of the Seminary garden, on the grand battery, from whence they were to run down to the Sally Port near Montcalms, there leap the wall & pass by the Canotrie into St Roc.

On the charge of these men, 2 of the Rebel Officers were sent on board Capt La forces arm'd schooner.[61]

The fogginess of the night made the garrison very watchful, every man lay down in his cloaths with his musket by his side.

1ST   In November last but few in this Garrison imagin'd that they shou'd see so many of their friends around them on this thrice welcome day.

Those who had never seen a siege painted to themselves scenes of desolation & distress.

During the winter the General's looks were narrowly watch'd; the tranquillity which appear'd in his countenance, added to the entire dependance we had on his military skill, dayly reliev'd us from former fears.

Much strength was added to the garrison by a short but eloquent address to the Militia assembled at the Chateau; the substance of it was, "that he had the names of the disaffected in his pocket book—he well knew the friends of Government, with these he wou'd answer with his life for the safety of the Garrison. For his part he was determin'd never to grace the triumph of the Rebels."

We all felt the force of his speech; it instill'd a noble spirit into many; the General, had he been in danger, wou'd have found a numerous band to conquer under him or fall by his side.

At 4 o clock this morning it began to snow & before 8 it lay 3 inches thick on the ground, at noon it began to clear up.

The Rebels fir'd red hot balls from the ferry, & from P Levy: they fire on the shipping; A shot enter'd the Cabin of the Fell, arm'd ship, shatter'd a boys leg, dangerously wounded a man by a splinter, & two more got bruises, tho slight.

A wretch of a Habitant paddled himself over from P Levy to day—he said that he came in, in consequence of Capt La Forces conference with him on the beach the other day.

He says the Rebels are 11000 strong, he wou'd fain have pass'd for a simple fellow, but the French people say, C'est un vrai coquin [He is a real rascal]—for that reason he is confin'd.

A very large bateau drifted down St. Charles' river to day, we sent out a canoe & brought it on shore.

2D   The night past was very clear & cold, it froze standing water a third of an inch thick; the Wind is N W & it freezes still.

The Rebels fir'd many red hot balls to day from the ferry

battery, some Chimneys & some roofs were a little hurt.[62]

We made a sortie at Port Louis for wood—near the old battery, behind fences & in the fields round about we found a great number of scaling ladders rather better made than the sample Arnold left behind him on the 31st Decr: but still too heavy & by far too short.

The General did not order them away in hopes that they wou'd attempt to use them we suppose; in that case a good account will be given of the besiegers.

At midnight rockets & a fire wheel were play'd off on the grand battery, & answer'd by rockets from the battery behind the Hotel Dieu.

3D   It was delightfully clear & serene in the night—this morning the air is Easterly. A fatigue party making a frize [tangled row] of thorn out of the ditch at Cape Diamond.

Three bodys of men were seen marching from the beach behind Wolfes cove towards the heights, 60 or 70 in each body—the 1st had red colours, the 2d blue, the 3d white: a number of bateaus attended them along shore. We take them to be part of Mr Thomas's reinforcement which Mr Rousseau pass'd at Still Water. The Rebels fire red hot balls to day, we threw some small shells from the N W end of St Roc into their battery at the ferry.

On the top of the tide between 9 & 10 o clock at night, (the moon shone very bright) a vessel was descried full sail, coming up to Town before the Wind; those who saw her wish'd one another joy of the 1st ship from England. A messenger was sent to inform the General that the first of the fleet was in sight—he order'd the artillery men to their guns—when she came within hail, it was ask'd from whence she came—no answer— hail'd again—still silent—the third hail was attended with a threat to sink her if no answer was made—she then gave a sheer on shore, & at that instant the batteries play'd briskly on her—in a moment she was all in a blaze, very near the beach & about 200 yds from the shipping in Cul de Sac. She was well garnish'd in all parts with shells, grenades, petards, pots a feu &c &c &c, they spent themselves very regularly:—she seem'd to have been well prepar'd; she must have done very great mischief if she had been steer'd into the Cul de Sac.

The instant that she sheer'd on shore a boat row'd from her with amazing speed.

It is suppos'd that this was Arnolds Brigantine which lay below: some say it was the Gaspey, & that she had pass'd the Town in a dark night. The whole city was under arms in a moment: no confusion appear'd, every body was cool & wishing that the Rebels might attack.

It is surprising that they chose to send her up in such clear weather: they are surely hard press'd: it is a hundred to one if they have not certain intelligence of ships of war being very near us—they had not a moment to lose.

The tide carried the fire ship down in a fine blaze; now & then we heard an explosion.[63]

The people under arms were dismiss'd with orders to be ready at a moments call.

4TH Wind still Easterly, the sky heavy, it rain'd till midday— a few shot from P Levy—Wind N W in the Evening.

5TH It froze hard last night, wind still N W & cold.

6TH There was frost last night with a gentle breeze at N E. About 4 o clock this morning guns were heard at a distance—we heard repeated reports nearer & nearer.

A woman came early to Palace Gate & inform'd the sentry that Mr Thomas with his reinforcement was arriv'd & that Mr Wooster was gone off, that they all appear in confusion, loading all the carts they can find with baggage arms &cc[64]

About 6 o clock a vessel appear'd turning P Levy to the inconceivable joy of all who saw her: the news soon reached every pillow in town, people half dress'd ran down to the Grand battery to feast their eyes with the sight of a ship of war displaying the Union flag.

She made signals of friendship & proved to be the Surprize Frigate commanded by Capt: Lindsay, part of the 29th Regiment with the Marines belonging to that Ship were immediately landed; the Isis & Sloop Martin arriv'd the same tide, their marines were also landed; the whole made about 200.[65]

The drums beat to arms; the different Corps assembled on the Parade.

It was there propos'd that the Volunteers of the British & Canadian Militia shou'd join the troops & Sailors to engage the Rebels on the plains; to their credit be it said that almost to a man both corps were anxious to be led to action.

The General at the head of about 800 men march'd out at 12 oclock; the little army extended itself quite across the plains making a fine appearance. The Rebels saw us very formidable.

A few shots were exchang'd by our advanc'd party & the rear guard of the enemy, their balls whistled over us without hurting a man—they fled most precipitately as soon as our field pieces began to play on their guard houses, & advanc'd posts, they left cannon, mortars, field pieces, muskets & even their cloaths behind them. As we pursued them we found the road strew'd with arms, cartridges, cloaths, bread, pork, &cc.

Their confusion was so great, their panic so violent, that they left orderly books & papers, which for their own credit shou'd not have been left. Look whatsoever way one wou'd, he saw men flying & loaden carts driving full speed.[66]

We took possession of their Gen: Hospital & of a guard house two miles beyond it, of Holland house, Mr Dupres &cc—there & at Sillerie we found provisions & artillery stores.

We return'd to Town about 4 o clock—the Surprise & Martin sail'd up the river to destroy the enemys craft. A guard was posted at the General Hospital in the evening.

7TH   Every thing was quiet in the night. This Morning the Priests from the adjacent Parishes came to town with chearful countenances to pay their respects to the Governor, & to render their devoirs to the Bishop; the steady & distinguish'd loyalty of the Canadian Clergy will ever redound to their honour.

All men entitled to the name of Gentlemen in this Country have behav'd like good & faithful subjects: many of them at the risk of their lives have shewn their attachment to the Kings

Government—not a few of the Nobless are now Prisoners with the Rebels; they voluntarily offer'd their services to oppose the Rebel invaders of Canada, & by the chance of war fell into the hands of the Rebels.

People are flocking into Town from all quarters—many of them hang their heads.

The Peasants come sneaking in with a few eggs or a pat of butter—conscious of their disloyal conduct, they are meanly submissive; ask any of them the price of what he has, "Ah mon cher Monsieur, says he, c'est a vous a faire le prix, ce qui vous plaira me contentera."[67]

Party's are detach'd all around. The Rebels abandon'd the Gaspey on the approach of our ships, she was half prepar'd as a fire ship, we found two other Vessels without any body on board.

The frigates fir'd on bateaus full of runaways; the turning of the tide unfortunately forc'd them to come to an anchor, & the bateaus row'd close to shore & got off.

To lighten their boats they inhumanly threw out many of their sick men upon the beach, some of them expir'd before our parties cou'd get to their relief, those objects of compassion whom we found alive were sent to the Gen: Hospital.[68]

Thus was the country round Quebec freed from a swarm of misguided people, led by designing men, enemies to the libertys of their country, under the specious title of the Assertors of American rights.

They preach'd up moderation in all cases; they gave us a few samples of it; their unremitted persecution of those who are attach'd to their sovereign, prove their great regard to the doctrine they preach.

These very moderate men whilst they were planning the invasion of this province were solemnly assuring the world that they wou'd not attempt to disturb the peace of Canada:—these peaceful protestations were intended to lull us asleep, for they were immediately follow'd by a hostile entry into this government; they took St Johns Chambly & Montreal, & block'd us up in Quebec in hopes of starving us into a compliance with their demands dictated by sedition & rebellion; their leader did every thing in his power to intimidate us; letters which he wrote to some of the principal Merchants in Town were taken in the possession of an old woman, he made them great promises, on condition that they wou'd not oppose his entry into Town. At the same time he wrote a letter to Gen: Carleton which for its originality ought to be recorded—it was conceiv'd in the following words—

Holland House, Decr: 6th

Sir,

   Notwithstanding the personal ill-treatment I have received at your hands—notwithstanding your cruelty to the unhappy Prisoners you have taken, the feelings of humanity induce me to have recourse to this expedient to save you from the Destruction which hangs over you. Give me leave Sir, to assure you, I am well acquainted with your situation. A great extent of works, in their nature incapable of defence, manned with a motley crew of sailors, the greatest part our friends; of citizens, who wish to see us within their walls & a few of the worst troops, who ever stiled themselves Soldiers. The impossibility of relief, & the certain prospect of wanting every necessary of life, should your opponents confine their operations to a simple Blockade, point out the absurdity of resistance. Such is your situation! I am at the head of troops accustomed to Success, confident of the right-ousness of the cause they are engaged in, inured to danger & so highly incensed at your inhumanity, illiberal abuse, and the ungenerous means employed to prejudice them in the mind of the Canadians; that it is with difficulty I restrain them till my Batteries are ready, from assaulting your works which afford them a fair opportunity of ample vengeance, and just retaliation. Firing upon a flag of truce, hitherto unprecedented, even among savages, prevents my taking the ordinary mode of communicating my sentiments. However, I will at any rate acquit my conscience. Should you persist in an unwarrantable defence, the consequences be upon your own head. Beware of destroying stores of any kind, Public or Private, as you have done at

*Montreal & in Three Rivers; If you do, By Heaven there will be
no mercy shewn.*

Richd: Montgomery,
Brigadier Gen. Cont. Army

His Excellency
Major General Carleton.
Quebec.[69]

Finding his threats & promises equally ineffectual he resolv'd to storm the city; but he was at a loss how to perswade his
Troops, as he call'd them, to march up to so desperate an attack;
Plunder he imagin'd wou'd be the strongest inducement to his
followers to attempt to get into Town; he sat himself down &
wrote the following Orders.

*Head Quarters Holland House
near Quebec 15th Decr. 1775.*

Parole—Connecticut
Countersign—Adams

*The General having in vain offer'd the most favourable
terms of accomodation to the Governor of Quebec, & having
taken every possible step to prevail on the inhabitants to desist
from seconding him in his wild scheme of defending the Town—
for the speedy reduction of the only hold possess'd by the
Ministerial Troops in this Province—The soldiers flush'd with
continual success, confident of the justness of their cause, &
relying on that Providence which has uniformly protected them,
will advance with alacrity to the attack of works incapable of
being defended by the wretched Garrison posted behind them,
consisting of Sailors unacquainted with the use of arms, of
Citizens incapable of Soldiers duty, & of a few miserable Emigrants*

The General is confident that a vigorous & spirited attack must be attended with success.

The troops shall have the effects of the Governor, Garrison, & of such as have been active in misleading the Inhabitants & distressing the friends of liberty, equally divided among them, except the 100th share out of the whole which shall be at the disposal of the General to be given to such soldiers as distinguished themselves by their activity & bravery, to be sold at public auction: the whole to be conducted as soon as the City is in our hands and the inhabitants disarm'd.[70]

Mr. Montgomery had his reputation as a Soldier at stake, he aim'd at the title of Conqueror of Canada:—The Congress had great dependance on him—he made the attack & met his fate.

The officers who had seen service made Soldiers of the Citizens.

Colonel M'Lean was indefatigable; he was here, there, & every where in a moment— in the worst of weather, as well as in the best; he was seen at all hours of the night as well as of the day.

Capt: M'Kenzie of the Hunter Sloop of War did duty as Major in the garrison—he was beyond conception active: the rebels batteries bear testimony of his assiduity, & of his skill in gunnery. He has much merit for bringing his Sailors under strict discipline—for Jack hates land service—he cannot brook restraint.[71]

Major Cox Lieut: Governor of Gaspey chearfully underwent the winters fatigue: he was remarkably zealous for the service. He engaging method of instructing the young soldier made his lessons to be much sought for.

Major Ecuyer who has likewise been long in the Army, took his turn of duty with the other field Officers; nothing was neglected by him to forward the service. By his example & by his precepts the British & Canadian Militia benefited not a little.

Major Lemaitre, major of brigade merits much applause for his good services.

Never was there a more active indefatigable careful officer than Major Faunce the Town Major.[72]

The Canadian Militia officers were likewise very assiduous

in their devoirs—in short the Officers in General did their duty, & the men follow'd their example.

The activity of individuals had a very visible effect on the whole.

If ever Emulation was conspicuous it was under General Carletons influence in the garrison of Quebec.

As the humanity of the following Proclamation, sets that goodness of heart for which the General is universally esteem'd in a proper point of view, it shou'd not here be omitted.

His enemies will love him; those who have fallen into his hands will bless heaven. Esteem & reverence must fill their souls, & many a prayer be put up for his preservation.

"Whereas I am inform'd that many of his Majesty's deluded subjects of the neighbouring Provinces labouring under wounds & divers disorders are dispers'd in the adjacent woods & Parishes, & in great danger of perishing for want of proper assistance; All Capts: & other Officers of Militia are hereby commanded to make diligent search for all such distress'd persons and afford them all necessary relief, & convey them to the General Hospital, where proper care shall be taken of them. All reasonable expenses which shall be incurr'd in complying with this Order shall be paid by the Receiver General.

And lest a consciousness of past offences shou'd deter such miserable wretches from receiving that assistance which their distress'd situation may require, I hereby make known to them, that as soon as their health is restor'd, they shall have free liberty to return to their respective Provinces.

Given under my hand & seal of arms at the Castle of St Louis in the City of Quebec this 10th day of May 1776 in the 16th year of the reign of our Sovereign Lord George the third.

By his excellency's   *Guy Carleton*
Command
H. T. Kramahé[13]

GOD SAVE THE KING

NOTES TO THE TEXT

1. This was probably a reference to the New York Provincial Congress, which assembled during 1775 to raise forces and supplies for the invasion of Canada. Smith, *Our Struggle for the Fourteenth Colony*, I, 182, 252-4.

2. After the capture of Fort Ticonderoga and Crown Point in May 1775, Benedict Arnold led a raid into Canada against Fort St. John. During the course of the raid, Arnold seized a boat carrying the Montreal mail. It contained a British government dispatch listing only two regiments of 717 men available to Governor Carleton, Smith, *op. cit.*, I, 230-1.

3. One of the principal colonial agents to whom Ainslie referred was John Brown, a Pittsfield, Massachusetts lawyer. In February 1775, Brown was sent by the Boston Committee of Correspondence into Canada, where he was to assess Canadian sentiments toward the Patriot cause. Brown travelled to Montreal, met with several sympathetic merchants, and sent back an optimistic dispatch in March recommending an attack on Fort Ticonderoga. Alden, *The American Revolution*, 1775-83, p. 46. Smith, *op cit.*, I, 91-103.

4. Ainslie gives unusually high praise to Lieutenant Governor Hector Theophilus Cramahé. His conduct before and during the defense of Quebec has generally been regarded as weak and vacillating. Alden, *op. cit.*, pp. 54-5. Smith, *op. cit.*, II, 5-10; Sheldon S. Cohen, "Lieutenant John Starke and the Defense of Quebec," *The Dalhousie Review* (Spring, 1967) XLVII, No. 1., 56-64.

5. The "old subjects" were those residents of Canada who had been born under the King of England. They had settled in Canada only since the French and Indian War and were differentiated from the "new subjects" or French Canadians. Thomas Walker and James Price, Montreal merchants, were two of the leading "old subjects" who were known for their pro-Patriot sentiments and their dealings with the American agent John Brown. French, *The First Year of the American Revolution*, pp. 146-7.

6. A reference to the Quebec Act, passed by Parliament in the spring of 1774. The Quebec Act established a limited government in Canada under the control of the Governor and a Crown-appointed Council. The Act left the Roman Catholic Church hierarchy and the aristocratic seigneurs with practically all their former economic and religious powers. For these reasons the Act had little support among the French Canadian habitants or the British "old subjects." American patriots disliked its favourable treatment toward Roman Catholicism as well as the fact that the Quebec Act extended the province's boundaries to the Ohio River. Alden, pp. 44-5.

7. Remember Baker was a member of Ethan Allen's Green Mountain Boys. During August 1775, Baker made a foray into Canada and was killed near Fort St. Johns in a skirmish with a party of Indians. Smith, I, 300-1.

8. Captain Tice was a Tory from Johnstown, New York. Smith, I, 331.

9. Major Campbell was Superintendent over all the Indians residing in Canada under British control. Smith, I, 177, 277.

10. Ethan Allen was held prisoner until May 6, 1778 when he was exchanged at New York for a British officer. See Gilbert H. Doane in *DAB* s.v. "Allan, Ethan." Major John Carden, formerly a captain in the Sixtieth (Royal American) Regiment of Foot. *A List of General and Field Officers . . . British and Irish Establishments*, 1770 (London, 1770).

11. In addition to his work as an apothecary and bookseller (see Introduction), Benedict Arnold had been involved in the horse-trading that went on between New England and Quebec and the West Indies. Ainslie, as a custom's collector, apparently remem-

bered him in this capacity. Smith, I, 117; Malcolm Decker, *Benedict Arnold, Son of the Havens* (New York, 1961), pp. 35, 37-8.

12. Major Joseph Stopford, Seventh Regiment of Foot, *List of General and Field Officers* . . . *British and Irish Establishments, 1775* (London, 1775). John Brown, the former agent of the Boston Committee of Correspondence (See Note 5) was at this time a lieutenant colonel in the Continental Army. Francis B. Heitman, *Historical Register of Officers of the Continental Army During the War of the Revolution, April, 1775 to December, 1783* (Washington, 1914), p. 125.

13. Colonel Allen McLean. The Royal Highland Emigrants was also known as His Majesties 84th Regiment. Literary and Historical Society of Quebec, *Historical Documents*, 7th Ser. (1905) p. 267.

14. Richard Prescott of the Seventh Regiment of Foot. Prescott had been newly promoted to the temporary rank of brigadier general when the American Revolution broke out. His regular rank was lieutenant colonel. French, pp. 423-4. *List of General and Field Officers,* . . . 1775; Ainslie was in error concerning Montreal. The Americans had taken the town on November 13. Smith, I, 481-3.

15. Ainslie's figures on the strength of the defenders were quite accurate. See Force, *American Archives*, 4th Ser., IV, 175; New York Historical Society, *Collections*, III, (1880), pp. 175-236; French, pp. 607-8.

16. "Bostonois" or "Bostonnais" was the derogatory term which French Canadians applied to English colonists in North America. Samuel E. Morison, *The Oxford History of the American People* (New York, 1965), p. 122.

17. On September 8 and September 14, Thomas Pownall, a member of the House of Commons and a former governor of Massachusetts, wrote Carleton that Russian mercenaries were being sent from England as reinforcements. Thomas Pownall to Governor Guy Carleton, *Canadian Archives*, B, 37, pp. 104, 106.

18. Major Jeremiah Dugan was a Canadian "old subject" who joined the patriot cause. During October 1775, he had assisted Colonel James Livingston in the capture of Fort Chambly and afterwards

he helped raise recruits among the habitants to join Montgomery's expedition against Quebec. The following year he was given command of a battalion of Rangers and aided General John Sullivan during his retreat from Canada. Heitman, *op. cit.,* p. 206; Smith, I, 401-2, 405, 426; II, 221-2, 395.

19. Holland House was described as "a long, high-peaked French mansion on a low but slight eminence." Smith, II, 99.

20. The Intendant's Palace was in the suburb of Palais, outside the Porte du Palais, in the Upper Town. For a good sketch of its ruins see "Historical Notes on the Defence of Quebec in 1775," *Transactions,* Literary and Historical Society of Quebec, (1876-7), Quebec, 1877, p. 22.

21. The American batteries had been secretly emplaced about 700 yards from the town. The American artillery consisted almost entirely of 6 and 12 pounders and, as Ainslie indicates, proved no match for the larger British guns. Smith, II, 102-6.

22. A cariole is a light horse-drawn sleigh. The Colonel Caldwell previously referred to was Major Henry Caldwell of the Royal Highland Emigrant Regiment serving in an upgraded rank. *List of General and Field Officers . . . 1775.*

23. The Récollet Monastery was located in the Upper Town across from Governor Carleton's headquarters in Governor's House. The Récollets were a branch of the Franciscan Order.

24. Saut au Matelot, a guardhouse and battery at the north end of the lower town. Pres de Ville, a guardhouse and battery at a narrow pass at the south end of the lower town.

25. Captain George Laws of the Royal Highland Emigrants. Literary and Historical Society of Quebec, *Historical Documents* 7th Ser., p. 267; Captain McDougal is not listed among the regular British officers who served during the seige.

26. Major John Nairne, formerly a Captain in the 78th Regiment of Foot. Lit. & Hist. Soc. of Quebec., *op. cit.*

27. Ainslie's account of the action was very accurate. From the American standpoint see the Journals of Jonathan Meigs and Isaac Senter. For the defenders, see the accounts of Henry Caldwell, John Starke, Hugh Finlay, and Sir John Hamilton. Also French,

pp. 614-20; Smith, II, 122-47. Captain Anderson was not listed as an officer either in the Regular Army or the Regular Navy. Correspondence, Public Record Office, London, England.

28. A cohorn was a small bronze mortar with handles mounted on a wooden block. It was used primarily for throwing light shells. A "royal" referred to a royal howitzer. Edward E. Curtis, *The Organization of the British Army in the American Revolution,* (New Haven, 1926), p. 7.

29. Captain John McPherson of Delaware was an aide-de-camp to General Montgomery. Captain Jacob Cheesman of New York was another aide-de-camp to Montgomery. Heitman, pp. 152, 375.

30. Major Return Jonathan Meigs of Connecticut. He later rose to the rank of full colonel after leading a successful raid against the British at Sag Harbor, Long Island in 1777. Heitman, p. 388.

31. At this time smallpox inoculation was generally performed by inoculating material from a skin lesion of a sick person into the skin of someone who was well. The inoculation was normally performed in isolation, sometimes after a preparatory treatment with mercurials and antimony. Francis R. Packard, *The History of Medicine in the United States* (Philadelphia, 1901), pp. 74-93.

32. Brigadier General David Wooster of Connecticut. The Canadians were proving reluctant to follow Wooster, but his main difficulty was a lack of monetary funds from Congress. Heitman, p. 606; Smith, II, 160-1.

33. Ainslie's estimate of the enemy in strength outside Quebec was slightly high. At this time the wounded General Arnold could command only a force of about five hundred Americans and two hundred Canadians. Two days after this entry Congress ordered reinforcements to Canada. French, pp. 626-7; Smith, II, 174-6.

34. The Canotrie was the harbor area of the Lower Town.

35. 1st Lieutenants Thomas Abbot and Jacob Scalch of the 4th Battalion Royal Regiment of Artillery. *List of General and Field Officers . . . 1775.* There is no record of a Captain Felton in the *Historical Register of Officers of the Continental Army.*

36. A number of the prisoners taken after Montgomery's abortive assault had been born in Great Britain. Some of these individuals were induced into taking an oath of allegiance to the Crown and agreed to serve under General Carleton's command until June, 1776. When a few of these new recruits violated their pledges and escaped over the walls to American lines, Carleton "disarmed and disuniformed" the remainder of the group and had them locked up in the artillery barracks. Smith II, 273-4.

37. Colonel James Clinton of New York. He was promoted to brigadier general on August 9, 1776. Heitman, p. 160; Major General Charles Lee of Virginia, Heitman, pp. 344-5; William Tryon had been governor of North Carolina and was governor of New York when the Revolution broke out. In October 1775, he sought refuge on a ship in New York Harbor and remained there until the following August, when troops under General William Howe arrived. See Leonard W. Labaree in *DAB* s.v. "Tryon, William". The rumors Ainslie reported were incorrect. On March 1, 1776, General Lee, whom Congress had previously ordered to take command of troops in Canada, was shifted to command American forces in the southern colonies. Smith, II, 206-7.

38. Sir John Johnson was the son of Sir William Johnson (1715-1774) the noted superintendent of Indian affairs and friend of the Iroquois tribes. Upon his father's death, Sir John fell heir to his father's title and lands and made his residence in the family mansion outside Johnstown, New York. He was a staunch Loyalist and roused Tory sentiment along the Mohawk River to such an extent that General Schuyler was forced to send a detachment to arrest him. Johnson, however, escaped and in June 1776, he joined Carleton's forces in Canada. See Wayne E. Stevens in *DAB* s.v. "Johnson, Sir John"; Smith, II, 165, 428.

39. The rumor of the disgruntled new commander was incorrect. General Wooster, however, was proving rather arbitrary in his rule over Montreal. Several residents, including one prominent Justice, were banished for suspected Loyalist sympathies. Smith, II, 228-34.

40. The Boston Massacre had occurred on March 5, 1770. It was

observed annually in much of New England at this time.

41. Ainslie was probably referring to the American Board of Customs Commissioners created in 1767.

42. This was apparently a quotation from the play *The Invader of His Country or The Fatal Resentment* by John Dennis (1657-1734), an English critic and dramatist. The play, first performed in 1719 at Drury Lane, bore a resemblance to Shakespeare's *Coriolanus*. In the Shakespeare play, Volumnia was the name of Coriolanus' mother.

43. Moses Hazen was appointed Colonel of the 2nd Canadian Regiment on January 22, 1776. He later rose to the rank of brigadier general. Heitman, p. 282; Edward Antill was appointed lieutenant colonel in Hazen's regiment, also on January 22, 1776. Prior to this, Antill had carried the news of Montgomery's disastrous assault on Quebec to the Continental Congress. Heitman, p. 72; Smith, II, 158-70.

44. Joseph François Cugnet was also detailed to command the company guarding the American prisoners. Lit. & Hist. Soc. of Quebec, *Hist. Docs.* (7th Ser.), pp. 270, 305.

45. The artillery pieces of the defenders included such large weapons as 32- and 42-pounders, and 13-inch mortars. Smith, II, 258.

46. The Dauphin Jail was described as a "dingy, gloomy sepulchre" with "heavy iron bars covering stone walls three feet thick." There was also a spiked wall twenty feet high surrounding the building. Smith, II, 277.

47. Captain Henry Laforce was listed as commander of an artillery company made up of loyal French Canadians. Lit. & Hist. Soc. of Quebec. *Hist. Docs.* (7th Ser.), pp. 270, 291.

48. Captain Humphrey Owen of the Seventh Regiment of Foot. *List of General and Field Officers . . . 1775.*

49. Ainslie was correct in his estimate of British firepower. It was not until March 11 that General Schuyler sent new artillery pieces, including two 24-pounders from St. Johns. These weapons did not arrive until the following month. Smith, II, 259.

50. The Englishman who gave away the escape plot was named

John Hall. He had deserted from the British forces in Boston the previous year. Smith, II, 289; For a good description of the prisoners' plan and its failure see Smith, II, 278-90.

51. General David Wooster had arrived from Montreal on this day, and at first displayed confidence that he could take Quebec. Smith, II, 255.

52. Merlons are the solid intervals between embrasures of a battlement parapet.

53. Father Lotbinière was reported to be the only priest who would offer absolution to Canadians who joined the patriot forces. Smith, II, 214, 217.

54. Captain-Lieutenant William Evans formerly of the 28th Regiment of Foot, Ireland. *List of General and Field Officers* . . . 1775.

55. A cavalier was a high structure inside a fort or bastion, which enabled troops to fire over the main parapet without interfering with its firing.

56. Point Levy or Levis was almost directly across from the Cul de Sac in the harbor of the Lower Town. It was in the Cul de Sac that British ships like the *Lizard* and *Hunter* were anchored.

57. At the end of March, the besiegers of Quebec numbered about 2500 but an estimated one-third of these men were unfit for duty. Although the enlistments of half of the total force were to expire on April 15, neither Arnold nor Wooster made any major move to re-enlist these men until the end of their service. The result was that on April 15, most of these troops, principally from New York, disregarded the last-minute pleas to re-enlist and laid down their weapons. Apparently the threat of force, plus new promises from General Wooster, prevented a general mutiny in the ranks. Some of the men, whose term of service had expired, were even induced to re-enlist. Smith, II, 310-12.

58. Lieutenant Colonel John Caldwell of the Eighth (the King's) Regiment of Foot. Caldwell at this time was in command of the British garrison at Detroit. He was stirring up the Indians of the Great Lakes region against the Americans, but it was not until May 12, 1776 that he ordered a force of British regulars, Can-

adians, and Indians to move against Montreal. *List of General and Field Officers* . . . 1776; Smith, II, 360, 67.

59. On March 17, 1776, British troops evacuated Boston and sailed to Halifax. Lord Stirling, or William Alexander of New Jersey, was at this time a brigadier general in the Continental Army. On August 27, 1776, he was taken prisoner at the Battle of Long Island. French, pp. 668-79. Heitman, p. 66.

60. On April 27, the Americans begun firing a brass 24-pounder, the largest gun they used during the siege. Ainslie was evidently reflecting some of the anxiety which existed among the defenders. It had been estimated the previous November that there was only enough food available until the middle of May and some provisions were already becoming scarce. Smith, II, 261-2, 267.

61. The American officers imprisoned in the seminary had not taken part in the enlisted men's schemes to escape in March. Their own plan of escape was planned afterward by Captains Samuel Lockwood and Simeon Thayer. The plan, however, was uncovered and collapsed in total failure. Smith, II, 291-3.

62. It was estimated that throughout the entire siege, the Americans fired about 780 cannon shots into the town of Quebec. Lit. & Hist. Soc. of Quebec. *Transactions 1876-7* (1877), p. 63.

63. The launching of the fire ship against British ships in the harbor of the Lower Town proved a desperate gamble and a dismal failure for the Americans. Smith, II, 314.

64. Lieutenant General John Thomas of the Massachusetts militia had arrived to take command of the American forces on May 1. On May 3, reinforcements from the Second Pennsylvania Regiment began to arrive. Two days later, however, Thomas received word of the British relief ships approaching Quebec. He immediately began to evacuate his sick and wounded troops. Smith, II, 309, 315-7.

65. Captain Francis Lindsay of the British Marines. The relief expedition was led by Sir Charles Douglas and the Twenty-Ninth Regiment of Foot was commanded by Colonel William Evelyn. *List of General and Field Officers* . . . 1776; Smith, II, 319.

66. For a description of the panic and the rout of American troops, see Smith, II, 320-2.

67. Ah, my dear sir, it is for you to set the price. I'll be content with what pleases you.

68. The American forces did not stop their retreat until they reached Deschambault, about 40 miles up-river from Quebec.

69. Most of the text of this letter is not included in the Ainslie diary. A copy of the original may be found in the Perceval-Maxwell Papers (T. 1023) at the Public Records Office of Northern Ireland, Law Courts Building, May Street, Belfast.

70. Montgomery to Carleton, December 15, 1775. Perceval-Maxwell Papers.

71. Captain Thomas McKenzie was commander of *H.M.S. Lizard,* one of the two Royal Navy ships which lay in Quebec Harbor during the siege. McKenzie, given the rank of major, led a detachment of seamen that helped defend the town. After the war he rose in rank and became an admiral in 1810, four years before his death. Midshipman George McKenzie, possibly a relative, also served on the *Lizard. H.M.S. "Lizard's" Log* (ADM 51/550), Public Record Office, London; Correspondence, Public Record Office.

72. Major Nicholas Cox, lieutenant governor of Gaspé, had served as an officer during the French and Indian War. Wilbur H. Siebert, "Loyalist Settlements on the Gaspé Peninsula," The Royal Society of Canada, *Transactions,* 3rd Ser. VIII, (1914), 401-5; Worthington C. Ford, *British Officers Serving in America* 1754-74 (Boston, 1894), p. 29;

    Major Simeon Ecuyer of the Canadian Militia and of the Sixtieth (Royal American) Regiment of Foot. *List of General and Field Officers* . . . 1776;

    Major Francis Le Maistre of the Seventh Regiment of Foot. *List of General and Field Officers* . . . 1776;

    Major Thomas Faunce had seen service as an officer during the French and Indian War. Ford, *op. cit.,* p. 38.

73. Cramahé retired from office on April 23, 1782 and died in England six years later. François J. Audet, *Canadian Historical Dates and Events,* 1492-1915 (Ottawa, 1917), p. 40. In 1778, Sir Guy Carleton was succeeded by Lieutenant General Haldimand as

governor of Quebec. Later, he served as commander of the British garrison in New York City until its evacuation on November 25, 1783. In 1786, with the title Baron Dorchester, he again returned to Quebec as governor. Carleton served in this capacity until July 1796 when he retired and returned to England. Sir Guy Carleton died at Stubbings near Maidenhead on November 10, 1808. See George F. R. Barker, *DNB* s.v. "Carleton, Guy."

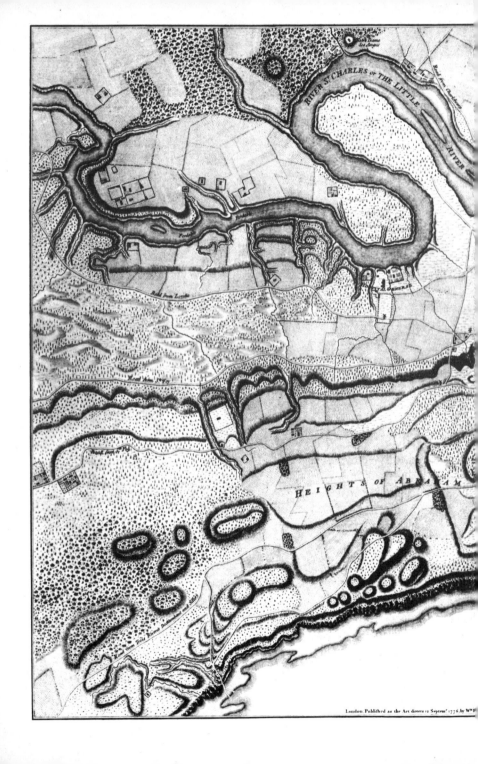

RIVER St CHARLES or THE LITTLE RIVER

HEIGHTS OF ABRAHAM

London Published as the Act directs 12 Septemr 1776 by Wm F